ARTHUR ASHE'S TENNIS CLINIC

By Arthur Ashe
Illustrations by Jim McQueen

A tennis MAGAZINE BOOK

Based on Tennis Magazine's "Tennis Clinic" Series

Published by Golf Digest/Tennis, Inc.
A New York Times Company
495 Westport Avenue
Norwalk, Connecticut 06856

Trade book distribution by
Simon & Schuster
A Division of Gulf + Western Industries, Inc.
New York, New York 10020

Second Printing
ISBN: 0-914178-44-X
Library of Congress: 80-84951
Manufactured in the
United States of America.

Original series designed for
Tennis Magazine by Michael Brent.
Book and jacket design by Dorothy Geiser.
Typesetting by
J&J Typesetters, Norwalk, Conn.
Printing and binding by
Kingsport Press,an Arcata Company.

To my tennis mentor, Dr. R. W. Johnson, and his son, Bobby.

INTRODUCTION

The instruction features of TENNIS magazine have always been of major importance to the magazine's readers. The great majority of the readers are players who, quite naturally, are constantly striving to improve their games. While there are many ways to learn the game and to improve, the basics of tennis are unchanging. That is why this book, the result of my Instruction Clinic series in TENNIS magazine, concentrates on the fundamentals of the game for the beginner, the improving and the better player.

This book is the product of three years of careful thought on my part in collaboration with the staff of TENNIS magazine. I wanted to illustrate the basics of the game in terms the average player can easily follow. Too much written tennis instruction is overly detailed and unnecessarily complicated. Here, the superb drawings of Jim McQueen blend with the straightforward text to explain the essentials of the game in a clear and entertaining way.

During my many discussions of this material with the magazine's editors, I came to the inescapable conclusion that the readers of this book will want to make their own simplifications of the game and personalize their own approaches to improvement. For that reason, I do *not* prescribe a "correct" way of playing tennis. There simply is no such thing. In these pages, I merely want to suggest, in easy to follow terms, what has worked for me and countless other players in the past. No matter what your level of play, you will inevitably end up with your own personal style.

In the magazine series and in this book, I have tried to show the strokes that can be used by most club level players. A player like Bjorn Borg, for example, has highly unorthodox strokes and serves, quite often, as an example of what *not* to do. Bjorn can hit the ball the way he does because he is an exceptional athlete but anyone who tried to copy him would find the going extremely rough.

On the other hand, Tracy Austin and Chris Evert Lloyd are excellent models of the conventional approach to ground strokes. While I would freely tell anyone to copy Tracy or Chris, I'd be very selective in recommending Borg's style to an improving player or a budding junior.

This book is meant to augment and not replace the teaching of your local professional. It is extremely difficult for anyone to teach himself tennis. In fact, I don't know of a single ranked player who has been completely self-taught. There simply is too much to learn about the game. Your teaching pro may disagree with some of the ideas presented here. That is just fine. There is no one way to learn or play the game.

A final word about your own game. Unless you started taking tennis lessons at a very early age, you will undoubtedly have some bad habits that a competent tennis teacher will spot and try to correct. In changing those faults, chances are, any one alteration will affect everything else in your play. So allow yourself enough time to gain confidence in your new strokes. Maybe you will even drop a match or two as you try to change. But if you are not willing to accept this temporary setback, you will not improve. Above all, improvement comes with much hard work, as I know all too well.

And speaking of hard work, I'd like to thank Jeff Bairstow, the managing editor of TENNIS magazine, for his patience and understanding as we compiled this book—and for putting up with too many soggy eggrolls during our many hours of collaboration.

Get your racquet back and follow through . . .

Arthur Ashe

CONTENTS

PART V | THE DOUBLES GAME

PART VI | TRAINING AND EQUIPMENT

PART I
BASICS OF THE GAME

1 ALL ABOUT GRIPS

1 **The grip is where your tennis begins.** Few players pay much attention to the way they hold the racquet and yet the grip has a lot to do with the way a person plays the game. For example, Bjorn Borg has an unusual forehand grip, often called a Western grip, which helps him hit the looping topspin shots that characterize his game. I doubt, though, that Borg ever gave much thought to his grip when he was a beginner.
On the other hand, I was taught to use a conventional Eastern forehand grip when I started playing at age 8. That grip was the foundation of the strokes in my repertoire. Each grip has its uses and its limitations. I could not play my game using a grip like that of Borg. So I'd like to take a look at the more common tennis grips and show you how they can affect your game.

2 **How to check your grip size.** Before we examine the different types of grips, take a moment to check that your racquet's handle is the right size for you. There are many ways to determine grip size but the two I prefer are shown in the drawings on the right. Hold the racquet normally with your fingers spread a little, as I'm doing here.
  You should be able to push the first finger of your other hand easily between the ends of your fingers and the fleshy part of your thumb (top right). Alternatively, check to see that your thumb and middle finger overlap from the first knuckle to the tips (bottom, right). You should use the largest grip size possible because that will help you feel the ball better and reduce the risk of arm or wrist injury.

3 **Start with the Eastern forehand grip.** I think beginners and intermediate players should start with the Eastern forehand and backhand grips because they will always produce a solid hit since the racquet face is almost square with the ball at impact. As your game improves, you can experiment with other grips. But fall back to the Eastern grips when you need to go back to the basics.

To get the Eastern forehand grip, you can either "shake hands" with the racquet handle (below, center) or start with your palm on the strings, move down to the handle and then grip it (below, left). In both cases, your fingers should be spread slightly and gripping the racquet firmly. For a proper Eastern forehand grip, the "V" formed by your thumb and first finger (below, right) should line up with the top right-hand edge of the handle as you look at it (left-hand edge if you're a lefty).

4 **Use the Eastern backhand grip.** If you use the Eastern forehand grip to hit a backhand ground stroke, your racquet face will be tilted back too much at impact and the ball will pop up in the air. So you must modify the grip to hit a backhand. Simply rotate the racquet handle about a quarter of a turn (below, left) until the "V" of your thumb and first finger is lining up with the top left-hand edge of the handle (assuming you are right-handed). The effect will be to make the racquet face more nearly vertical as you hit the ball (below, right) for a relatively flat shot. You can still hit topspin shots with either of the Eastern grips simply by taking the racquet back low and finishing high. So the Eastern grips offer the average player all the versatility he or she requires.

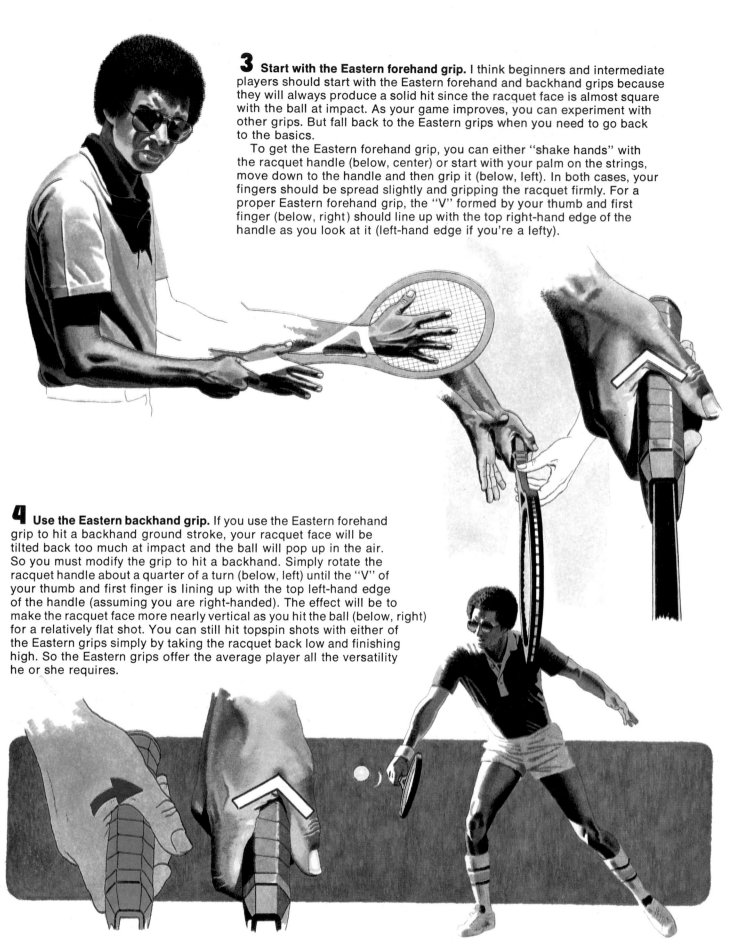

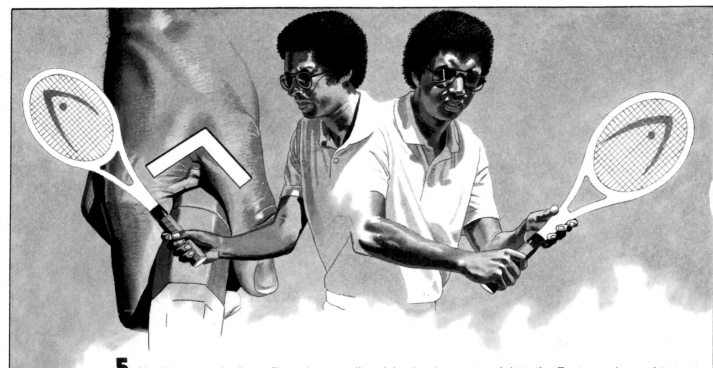

5 **Modify your grip for volleys.** I generally advise beginners to stick to the Eastern grips and to switch from forehand to backhand even when hitting volleys. However, as you improve and you begin to play more at the net, you should try to use one grip for both these volleys because there just isn't enough time to switch between shots.

I advocate the Continental grip which is midway between the Eastern forehand and backhand grips so the "V" is in the center of the top of the handle (top left). With this grip you can hit either volley without a change. Some players favor a volleying grip that is more to the backhand side, others, one that is more to the forehand side. It's all a matter of personal preference. Experiment and find the one that suits your strokes best.

6 **Try a Western grip for excessive topspin.** In my clinics at the Doral in Miami, I'm often asked about the Western grip—the one used by Borg. With this grip, the hand is even farther behind the handle (near right) than it is with the Eastern forehand grip. For young players, the Western is often a natural grip which feels quite comfortable. It's possible to hit the ball quite firmly provided the racquet face is kept vertical or tilted back slightly at contact with the ball. However, there's a strong tendency for the racquet face to close (tilt forward), which means that the ball is often hit into the net. Borg has an immensely strong wrist and impeccable timing, so he can put the Western grip to good use to hit those looping topspin forehands. Incidentally, Borg uses a Continental grip for his two-handed backhand because that helps him take the racquet back low for topspin on that side.

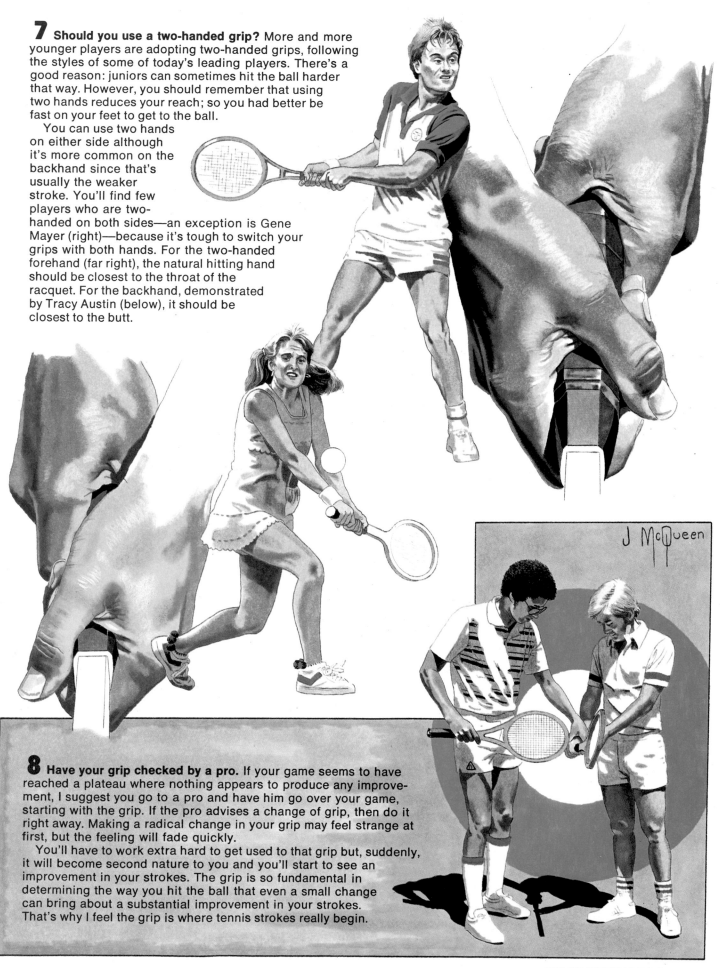

7 **Should you use a two-handed grip?** More and more younger players are adopting two-handed grips, following the styles of some of today's leading players. There's a good reason: juniors can sometimes hit the ball harder that way. However, you should remember that using two hands reduces your reach; so you had better be fast on your feet to get to the ball.

You can use two hands on either side although it's more common on the backhand since that's usually the weaker stroke. You'll find few players who are two-handed on both sides—an exception is Gene Mayer (right)—because it's tough to switch your grips with both hands. For the two-handed forehand (far right), the natural hitting hand should be closest to the throat of the racquet. For the backhand, demonstrated by Tracy Austin (below), it should be closest to the butt.

8 **Have your grip checked by a pro.** If your game seems to have reached a plateau where nothing appears to produce any improvement, I suggest you go to a pro and have him go over your game, starting with the grip. If the pro advises a change of grip, then do it right away. Making a radical change in your grip may feel strange at first, but the feeling will fade quickly.

You'll have to work extra hard to get used to that grip but, suddenly, it will become second nature to you and you'll start to see an improvement in your strokes. The grip is so fundamental in determining the way you hit the ball that even a small change can bring about a substantial improvement in your strokes. That's why I feel the grip is where tennis strokes really begin.

2 FUNDAMENTALS FOR A BETTER FOREHAND

1 **Develop a dependable stroke.** I'd be willing to bet that more than 90 percent of all players start out by hitting forehands. It's a familiar motion to them —a lot like swinging a baseball bat, for instance. And it quickly becomes the bedrock of their games, the stroke to call on at critical times and to fall back on when other strokes fail them. So a reliable forehand is a vital ingredient in every player's game. It's important, thus, to learn the stroke properly from the start and to avoid slipping into bad habits as your game develops.

2 **Use an Eastern Grip.** I recommend the full Eastern forehand grip (see below), which puts most of your hand directly behind the handle so you can grip firmly and hit the ball solidly. An easy way to check your forehand grip is to place your hitting hand on the strings of the racquet and then slide your hand down the shaft (see below) until you can wrap your fingers around the grip. The "V" formed by your thumb and forefinger should line up with the top right edge of the handle (if you're a right-hander).

3 **Be ready to move.** When you are playing at the baseline, you must be alert and prepared to move quickly either sideways for wide balls or toward the net for shorter balls. So I suggest that you wait poised like a boxer with your weight on the balls of your feet but in perfect balance. Your knees should be bent and your feet a little more than shoulder-width apart. Keep your racquet out in front of you, about waist high, ready to start your swing to either side. If, like most club players, you are better on the forehand side, you should wait with a forehand grip and make a quick grip change if the ball comes to the backhand side.

4 **Turn your shoulders.** The most common failing among players on ground strokes is not getting their racquets back quickly enough. So as soon as you realize that you are about to hit a forehand, start your racquet head moving back. Turn your upper body first so that your racquet head, arm and shoulder move as one unit (see far right).Then, keep the racquet head moving for a full backswing (see near right). As you start your backswing, begin stepping or running into position to make your shot.

5 **Get your racquet all the way back.** At the end of your backswing, your racquet should be pointing almost directly at the back fence with the handle nearly parallel to the ground and the racquet head perhaps a little higher than your waist. Freeze your racquet during practice occasionally to make sure you're getting it back as far as you should. A full backswing permits you to take a strong cut at the ball— not a half-hearted one. And don't lean to the rear in an attempt to get your racquet all the way back. You should keep your weight slightly forward, ready for the swing toward the ball. At the completion of the backswing, pivot on your rear foot so you can push off and transfer your weight all the way forward (see the near drawing).

6 **Step out to meet the ball.** To hit a powerful forehand, you must put your weight into the shot. And you can do that only by stepping out to meet the ball as it comes toward you. So you should first get sideways to the ball as you take your racquet back. That means pivoting on your rear heel as you get close to the expected line of flight of the ball (top, far left). Then, you should step toward the ball as you start your forward swing (top, left), firmly planting your front foot at about a 45-degree angle to the base-line before you actually hit the ball. That way, you'll be moving your weight forward as you hit through the ball (center, left). When you complete your hit, all your weight should be on your front foot. But maintain proper balance by keeping the toes of your back foot on the ground.

7 **Concentrate on hitting the zone.** The most critical part of your forehand swing is, as you'd expect, the hitting zone where your racquet should be in contact with the ball. For most players, the hitting zone starts in front of the rear hip and continues to the point where the racquet is almost level with the front foot (see right). Your objective should be to keep the ball on the strings for as much of that hitting zone as possible—by hitting smoothly through the ball, as the pros say. The longer you can keep the ball on the strings, the more control you will have over your shot. So you should really concentrate on the ball in that hitting zone. You must try to watch it intently, although it's unlikely that you will be able to see the actual contact.

J McQueen

8
Finish your follow-through with a vertical racquet face. From the hitting zone, move the racquet into a full follow-through to complete the shot. Let your arm swing around your body until the racquet finishes high in front of you with the racquet face almost vertical (left). The back of your hand should be pointing to the side fence so that you do not roll your racquet over during the shot. That way, you'll be sure you hit either a flat shot—or one with a little natural topspin. If you roll your wrist too much in an attempt to put excessive spin on the ball, you'll probably hit a weak and erratic shot. I also like to exhale as I follow through because that helps my concentration. You might like to try that, too. Simply exhale sharply like a karate expert.

9 **Hitting on the run.** If the ball is coming relatively close to you on your forehand side, it's a fairly simple matter to skip smartly sideways to get into position to hit the ball. But on a wide forehand, you'll actually have to run for the ball. So you may have little time to position yourself and hit smoothly. To make the best shot possible, take big running strides to get close to the ball and, then, smaller, rapid steps to get into final position. Your racquet should be going back as you run and your last step should be toward the ball with your forward foot. You should not be running as you hit the ball because your body weight will be going sideways and you'll keep on going after you've made contact. So pause sufficiently to plant your rear foot before you push off to transfer your weight forward into the shot. If your weight's on your front foot after making contact, you'll be in good shape to recover and get back into position for the next shot.

3 BASICS OF THE BACKHAND

1 **The key to a solid stroke.** Like many professional and advanced players, my strongest ground stroke is the backhand. That's largely because the backhand is a more natural stroke since the arm opens up across your body instead of closing around it as it does on the forehand. And in almost all cases, those who hit the backhand well have developed the stroke by putting more time and effort into it. I believe that my success with the stroke stems from the fact that I learned as a child to get my racquet back early.

2 **Use a proper backhand grip.** If you tried to use a conventional Eastern "shake-hands" forehand grip on your backhand side, you'd find that most of your shots would sail too high over the net because the racquet face would be tilted back too much. So for a clean stroke, you must change your grip in order to get the racquet face more nearly perpendicular to the flight of the ball. For a right-hander like me, that means rotating the racquet head about a quarter turn to the right so that the left edge of the top of the handle is lined up with the "V" formed by my thumb and first finger (see left).

3 **Turn your shoulders first.** For the early backswing that's so essential to a good backhand you must do two things. First, you have to sharpen your sense of anticipation so you can make a quick decision to take your opponent's ball on your backhand side. And secondly, you should turn your shoulders as soon as you make your choice. A rapid shoulder turn will get you sideways to the ball and will automatically start your racquet moving back for that early backswing. Of course, you may also have to move into position to make your shot. If that's the case, turn your shoulders as you move. By the time you arrive at the point where you're going to hit the ball, your racquet should be fully back.

4 **Get your racquet all the way back.** Draw your racquet back as far as you can. Don't pull it part of the way back, pause and then swing forward; that kind of halfway stroke will produce a half-hearted shot. For power and consistency, take a full swing at the ball—using one smooth motion from the backswing to the forward swing to the follow-through. My racquet head is relatively high at the end of the backswing because I have a looping action on my backhand. Other players may prefer a straight backswing which puts the racquet about waist-high at the completion of the backswing. How you take your racquet back is much less important than getting the racquet all the way back and bringing it forward so that the head is rising slightly through the hitting zone (see the next page).

5 **Bring your racquet up to meet the ball.** Since most backhand ground strokes are made close to or behind the baseline, the ball will have to travel nearly the full length of the court to get the kind of depth you should have on your shot. That's not too hard to do—provided you hit the ball high enough over the net. But a net-skimmer will have to be hit exceptionally hard to go deep into your opponent's court. You should hit the ball so that you lift it several feet over the net. You can do that more easily if you bring your racquet forward on a gently rising plane to meet the ball, and if you hit it with a slightly open face—that is, with the racquet face tilted back a bit.

6 Keep the ball on your strings through the hitting zone. Make contact with the ball just in front of your forward foot and keep the ball on your strings for as long as possible. The racquet face should travel on a straight upward line through the hitting zone in the direction you want the ball to go. If you're trying to hit the ball crosscourt, make contact a little farther out in front. But if you're trying to send the ball down the line, make contact a little later, closer to your forward foot. In either case, you'll increase your accuracy if you keep the ball on the strings for as long as you can. So at impact, don't swing the racquet head around; instead, push it out in front along the line that you want the ball to go. And as you hit through the ball, your weight should be moving forward to add extra power to the shot. Hitting through the ball with proper weight transfer will give you a powerful backhand.

7 Meet the ball firmly. I've noticed that many club players, because they seem to have a fear of the backhand, try to get rid of the ball as quickly as possible. So instead of hitting through the ball, they slap at it. The problem often seems to be that the player leads with his wrist. Thus, he has to swing the racquet head around in a fishtailing motion, using his wrist and forearm or even just the wrist. When you hit a backhand, your racquet, wrist and forearm should move as one unit until the ball leaves your racquet.

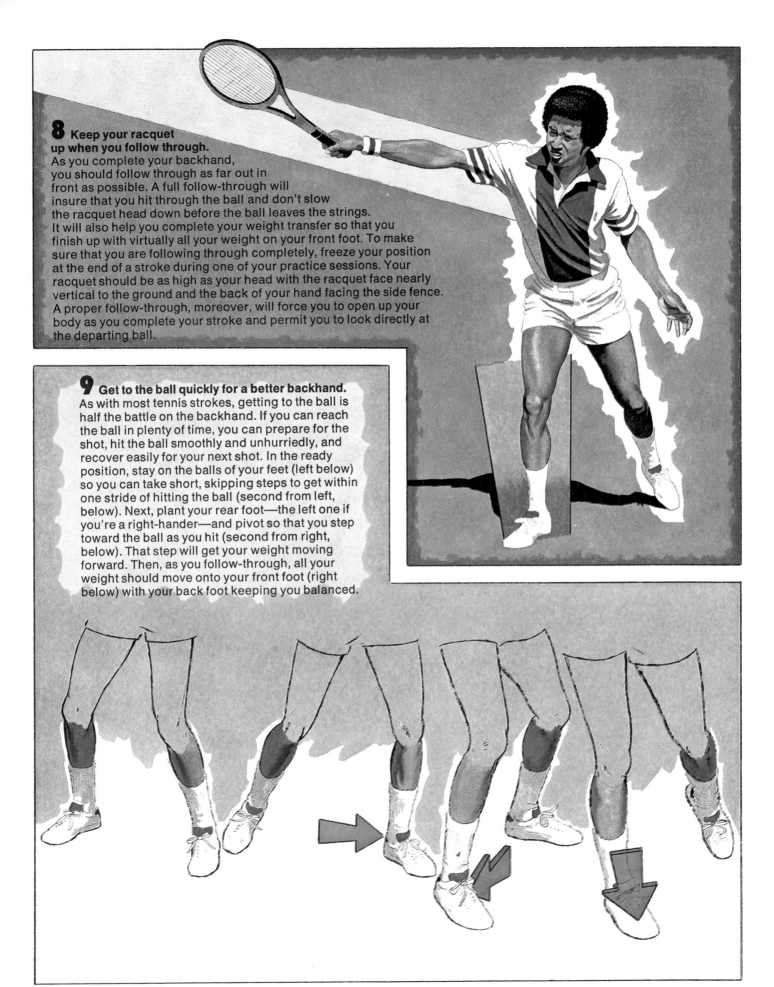

8 **Keep your racquet up when you follow through.**
As you complete your backhand, you should follow through as far out in front as possible. A full follow-through will insure that you hit through the ball and don't slow the racquet head down before the ball leaves the strings. It will also help you complete your weight transfer so that you finish up with virtually all your weight on your front foot. To make sure that you are following through completely, freeze your position at the end of a stroke during one of your practice sessions. Your racquet should be as high as your head with the racquet face nearly vertical to the ground and the back of your hand facing the side fence. A proper follow-through, moreover, will force you to open up your body as you complete your stroke and permit you to look directly at the departing ball.

9 **Get to the ball quickly for a better backhand.**
As with most tennis strokes, getting to the ball is half the battle on the backhand. If you can reach the ball in plenty of time, you can prepare for the shot, hit the ball smoothly and unhurriedly, and recover easily for your next shot. In the ready position, stay on the balls of your feet (left below) so you can take short, skipping steps to get within one stride of hitting the ball (second from left, below). Next, plant your rear foot—the left one if you're a right-hander—and pivot so that you step toward the ball as you hit (second from right, below). That step will get your weight moving forward. Then, as you follow-through, all your weight should move onto your front foot (right below) with your back foot keeping you balanced.

1 The rise of the two-handers. Two-handed hitters seem to be everywhere these days —in the public parks, in private clubs and, of course, in both men's and women's pro events. But there's nothing new about the two-handed style; Pancho Segura, for example, was walloping two-handed forehands in the 1940's, long before I ever picked up a tennis racquet. Like all of my contemporaries, I was taught to hit the orthodox way with the same hand off both sides. Nowadays, youngsters are often encouraged to use two hands to compensate for a lack of grip and arm strength, particularly on the backhand side.

Many players continue to use two hands into their adult playing careers and that's why we have such a great crop of two-handers today. Such players as Chris Evert Lloyd, Jimmy Connors, Tracy Austin, Gene Mayer and Bjorn Borg started young with their two-handers and have refined them into powerful weapons.

2 When two hands help. I want to emphasize at the start that two-handed strokes are not for everyone. If you can hit passable one-handed ground strokes, then you should work on improving them rather than attempting to switch to a two-handed stroke. If you have a weak grip, however, then two hands will give you the extra strength and support you need to hit a powerful shot. A youngster will often have trouble gripping the racquet with one hand on the backhand side because the hand is pulling the racquet through rather than pushing it forward. Thus, the extra hand can go behind the handle for additional support, as Tracy Austin demonstrates so well above.

3 Begin with the basics. When you start working on a two-handed backhand, concentrate on the basics. Your models ought to be Tracy Austin or Chris Evert Lloyd (left) who both hit through the ball with a relatively flat stroke. Don't imitate the looping two-hander of Bjorn Borg until you have mastered the basic flat backhand. You'll get maximum power on your backhand if you take the racquet almost straight back and then swing forward with the racquet head on a plane that's almost parallel to the ground. In fact, the use of two hands allows you to keep the swing flatter for a longer period than you can with one hand. It means the ball stays on the strings for a fraction of a second more. And that's what adds the extra power—more ball and string contact. Your follow-through should be out and up as with the one-handed shot. Indeed, some two-handers let go with the other hand after hitting the ball to avoid a cramped follow-through. Either way is fine.

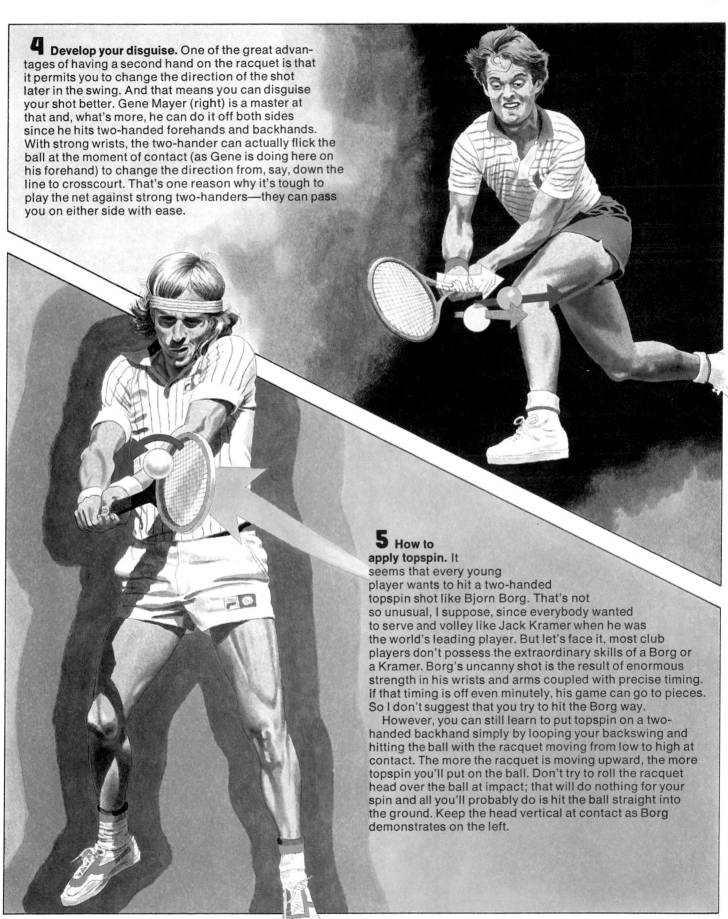

4 Develop your disguise. One of the great advantages of having a second hand on the racquet is that it permits you to change the direction of the shot later in the swing. And that means you can disguise your shot better. Gene Mayer (right) is a master at that and, what's more, he can do it off both sides since he hits two-handed forehands and backhands. With strong wrists, the two-hander can actually flick the ball at the moment of contact (as Gene is doing here on his forehand) to change the direction from, say, down the line to crosscourt. That's one reason why it's tough to play the net against strong two-handers—they can pass you on either side with ease.

5 How to apply topspin. It seems that every young player wants to hit a two-handed topspin shot like Bjorn Borg. That's not so unusual, I suppose, since everybody wanted to serve and volley like Jack Kramer when he was the world's leading player. But let's face it, most club players don't possess the extraordinary skills of a Borg or a Kramer. Borg's uncanny shot is the result of enormous strength in his wrists and arms coupled with precise timing. If that timing is off even minutely, his game can go to pieces. So I don't suggest that you try to hit the Borg way.

However, you can still learn to put topspin on a two-handed backhand simply by looping your backswing and hitting the ball with the racquet moving from low to high at contact. The more the racquet is moving upward, the more topspin you'll put on the ball. Don't try to roll the racquet head over the ball at impact; that will do nothing for your spin and all you'll probably do is hit the ball straight into the ground. Keep the head vertical at contact as Borg demonstrates on the left.

6 **Use one hand for extra reach.** Two-handed shots do reduce your ability to get to wide balls because the trailing arm limits your reach. For example, there's no way I could get my racquet on the ball at the left if I had a two-handed backhand. You have to be closer to the ball when you use two hands than you do with one in order to hit an effective shot. That means you need to be either fast on your feet so you can get into position quickly (like Bjorn Borg) or be prepared to use one hand occasionally for the very wide balls (like Jimmy Connors who can hit a one-handed backhand, too). Among the pros, we say that you have to be one-half step faster to hit a wide shot with two hands. That may not sound like a lot, but it can spell the difference between hitting the ball or missing it.

7 **Go with two hands only on one side.** Unless you have a really weak grip, I think you ought to restrict your use of two hands to one side. It is perfectly possible to use two hands on both sides as Gene Mayer and Hans Gildemeister (right) do. The right-hander's two-handed forehand is exactly like the lefty's two-handed backhand (compare Gildemeister here with Jimmy Connors on the opposite page) and, thus, it is usually a powerful shot with all the normal two-handed advantages.

The problem comes on the other side—in Gildemeister's case, for example, on his two-handed backhand. There's no time to transpose his hands and assume a proper two-handed backhand grip. So he keeps his hands in the same position and the result is that he hits off the backhand side with his arms crossed (see inset), producing an awkward-looking stroke with the disadvantages of a restricted reach and an abbreviated swing. Gildemeister ovecomes that because he's developed strong wrists and forearms.

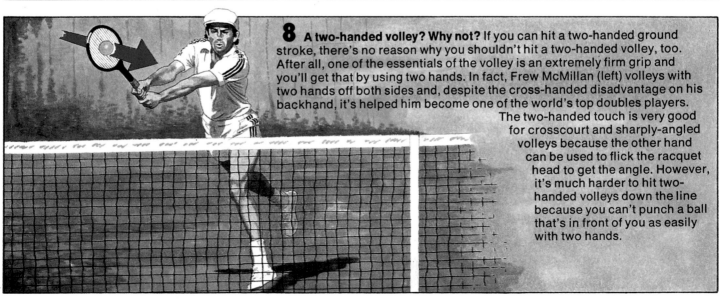

8 **A two-handed volley? Why not?** If you can hit a two-handed ground stroke, there's no reason why you shouldn't hit a two-handed volley, too. After all, one of the essentials of the volley is an extremely firm grip and you'll get that by using two hands. In fact, Frew McMillan (left) volleys with two hands off both sides and, despite the cross-handed disadvantage on his backhand, it's helped him become one of the world's top doubles players. The two-handed touch is very good for crosscourt and sharply-angled volleys because the other hand can be used to flick the racquet head to get the angle. However, it's much harder to hit two-handed volleys down the line because you can't punch a ball that's in front of you as easily with two hands.

9 **Recognize the vulnerabilities.** Many two-handed players are strongest off the two-handed side so, when it's the backhand side, the usual premise in club play of hitting to the backhand doesn't apply. One obvious alternative is to attack the forehand if that, indeed, is weaker. But any two-hander is vulnerable to balls hit straight at him or her. Just as two-handers have to be faster to get to wide balls, they also have to move quickly to back away from balls aimed right at them in order to use those two-handed shots effectively.

As you see above, when the ball is hit almost directly at him, Jimmy Connors is forced to lean away from the ball so he can get his two-handed backhand on it. Consequently, he'll hit the ball awkwardly and without his customary power. Two-handers can have particular problems with serves that come straight at them—especially if a serve kicks relatively high in the air. The high ball aimed at the body will often produce a weak reply.

10 **Watch out for lobs.** I'm not quite sure why, but most two-handed players are susceptible to what I call "teaser" lobs to both sides. These are offensive lobs that barely clear the opponent's racquet (like the one that Jimmy Connors is struggling for on the right) or high balls that just can't be reached with the two-handed backhand. I suppose that two-handed players become so used to hitting with two hands that their one-handed shots are weak by comparison.

So my defense against two-handers would be to hit balls to the weaker side, shots directly at the body (as I suggested above) and a few crafty lobs. That plan will not allow the two-hander to take advantage of his or her powerful stroke.

J McQueen

5 MAKE THE LOB WORK FOR YOU

1 **A neglected shot.** The lob is by far the most under-estimated and, therefore, most underused stroke in the game. Few players, even among the pros, appreciate its full effectiveness. They seldom take the time to practice it and, as a result, they're almost afraid to use it in a match. That's a shame because the lob can be really effective in many different situations in a match and isn't a tough shot to hit. To help you make it an efficient part of your game, I'll show you first when you can use a lob and then how to hit the stroke. I'm not going to get into the differences between the defensive lob (a high, arcing shot) and the offensive lob (which takes a lower trajectory) because I think a proper offensive lob is too difficult for the club player. You should concentrate simply on hitting a good lob, which can be high or low depending on the situation.

2 **Getting out of a tight spot.** For the average player, the most important time to use a lob is when you are pulled out of position and you need a shot that will give you time to recover and get back into the point. For example, say that a player with a good slice serve pulls you wide in the deuce court. You can make the best of the situation by returning the serve with a lob that should go high and deep. The height will give you time to hustle back to the center of the baseline and the depth will keep your opponent back on his baseline. So when you are in a tight spot, hit a lob that goes high and deep—and preferably crosscourt to give yourself the largest margin for error.

3 **Discouraging the net rusher.** Another opportune time to put up a lob is when you're facing an opponent who consistently charges the net and is hard to pass with shots hit to the side of him. Send up a lob that will clear the top of his outstretched racquet and drop behind him—possibly for a winner. This lob should go deep, but it won't necessarily need the height required when you're just trying to stay in the point. It's a good idea, by the way, to lob the net rusher early in your match to show him that he's taking a chance by coming too close to the net. The farther you can keep him from the net, the less likely he is to win the point. So by using your lob to beat a net-rusher, you'll be keeping him honest.

4 **Tiring out an opponent.** If you figure that you're in for a long, closely-fought match, you can wear your opponent down by sending up lob after lob. That will force him to chase down the ball and hit overheads. Hitting a lot of overheads, particularly from deep in the court, is really fatiguing and your opponent is likely to wilt long before the end of the match. Even if he recognizes your ploy and returns your lobs with ground strokes, he'll still get weary. That's because a ball that drops as steeply as a lob has no pace or forward momentum on it and has to be hit hard for an effective return. So you can use a lob to tire your opponent even when he's playing in the backcourt.

5 **Prepare as you would for a ground stroke.** Keep in mind that a lob is basically a ground stroke —but one that often has to travel not only the length of the court but must also rise many feet in the air. That means you must hit the ball just as hard as you do other ground strokes. So prepare with a full backswing. In fact, take the racquet back with the same motion that you'd use for a forehand or backhand drive so your opponent can't tell what kind of shot you are going to hit until you contact the ball. If you have enough time, turn sideways to the ball, take your racquet all the way back and step toward the ball as you begin your forward swing.

6 **Anchor your back foot.** The key to hitting a solid lob is to control the ball. Stroke through the ball and transfer your weight forward as you would with any other ground stroke. The mistake many players make is to hit the ball while leaning backward so that it flies almost straight up in the air and either falls short or doesn't even cross the net. So as you start your forward swing, step toward the ball and get your weight moving forward by pushing off your back foot. But keep that back foot anchored to the ground or you'll lose your balance and hit a poor shot. As you meet the ball, your weight should be moving onto your front foot with your back foot used as a stabilizing anchor.

7 **Use a firm wrist.** I've noticed that many club players have a tendency to flick at the ball, using excessive wrist action, when they try to hit a lob after scrambling for the ball. Nothing could be worse. A wristy shot will pop right off your racquet, and you'll not only lack control of the shot, you'll also get little power into it. You have to keep your wrist firm as you make contact with the ball. Simply grip the racquet tightly and keep your wrist firm so that you can stroke solidly through the ball. That way, you'll be able to lift the ball high and make it go deep into your opponent's court.

8 **Get under the ball at contact.** Swing your racquet forward, just as you do for a normal ground stroke. But just before contact, drop your racquet below the level of the ball (keeping the shaft parallel to the ground so you don't scoop the shot). At the same time, open your racquet face by tilting it back slightly. Then, lift the ball in the air by bringing the racquet face up and forward, keeping it perpendicular to the expected line of flight of your shot. The slightly open racquet face will give you more control by putting a little underspin on the ball. Bob Hewitt (right), among the great doubles stars of recent years, is one pro who has mastered the lob and uses it to telling effect. He lobs effectively because he keeps a firm wrist and controls the position of his racquet head so well.

9 **Swing as high as you can.**
A full follow-through is absolutely
essential on the lob. So after impact,
move the racquet out in front of you as
high as you can in the direction that the
ball is going (as Ken Rosewall and I are
doing in the drawings on the right). Rosewall's
lob has always been excellent because it's a
simple and smoothly executed stroke with a
complete follow-through. Many players, though,
seem to be reluctant to follow through as much
as they should, evidently for fear of hitting the ball
too far. But if you cut your swing short, the
chances are that the ball will be a harmless floater
with little height or depth. In other words, you'll be
serving up a ball that your opponent can probably
knock into the next county. A full follow-through,
on the other hand, will make you keep your ball on
the strings longer and, thus, give you better
control. You'll lift the ball in the air, and get the
height and depth you want.

6 HOW TO PERFECT YOUR BALL TOSS

1 **The key to a better serve.** When you mess up a forehand or a volley, the reason may be at least partly because your opponent hit you too difficult a ball. But when you mess up a serve, there's only one person at fault: you. The serve is the one shot where you're completely in control, where you have no one to blame but yourself if you don't hit it right. To serve well, you've got to begin by launching the ball properly. The ball toss, in fact, is the cornerstone of a solid, reliable serve. If you toss the ball to the right spot every time, you'll be rewarded with a solid, consistent delivery. But if you don't—if the ball is too low one time and too far out in front of you the next—you'll be punished with an erratic serve, to say nothing of an embarrassing number of double faults. So let's examine the way to develop the dependable ball toss you need for an effective serve.

45°

2 **How to prepare properly.** For a consistent toss, the first thing to do is to get yourself comfortable. Don't rush your serve; there's no hurry and your opponent isn't going any place. In singles, you should stand close to the center mark with your feet a little more than shoulder width apart. Your front foot should be at about 45 degrees to the baseline, putting your upper body at roughly the same angle. Adjust your position like a golfer preparing to address the ball until you feel comfortable. Bounce the ball a couple of times if you feel that helps. When you are quite ready, start your motion with your racquet in front of you, cradled by the hand that's holding the ball. Your hands should always start from the same position to help the rhythm of the motion.

3 **Let your arms move together.** I like to think of the serve as a three-piece action: tossing the ball; raising the racquet; and swinging at the ball. However, the first two should be done simultaneously; that is, you should toss the ball and raise your racquet at the same time. So from the ready position, your arms should drop together and then come up as though you were describing separate halves of a large circle. *Bring both arms up at the same speed* and you won't have any problems timing your serve. Make sure, though, that your arms go all the way down before they start up again. Practice this simultaneous swing with a ball and racquet, but without letting go of the ball. Repeat it until you develop a smooth action —like a swimmer doing the backstroke.

4 **Move your weight forward.** For a really powerful serve, you have to put your weight into the shot. But don't wait to do that just as you swing up to hit the ball. *Your weight transfer must start with your ball toss.* If you are relatively new to the sport, I suggest you start with your weight on your back foot. That way, you can shift your weight forward as you lift the ball in front of you. Most better players, however, prefer to start with the weight on their front foot so they can rock back slightly as their arms come down to begin the serving motion. Of course, the end result is the same: your weight moves into the serve as you start to toss the ball. The rocking motion has another effect, too; it lets you swivel your hips away from the net so that your body is coiled and ready to be thrown into the serve. It's almost like the hip movement of a golfer as he swings into a drive.

5 **Reach up to release the ball.** Although we call the action a "toss," you should not throw the ball into the air. The idea is to reach. The momentum from this motion should be sufficient to take the ball high enough in the air for you to swing your racquet and make proper contact. If you are moving into your serve, your body will also be moving up to give you a little extra reach before you release the ball. The higher you release the ball, the more accurate your toss will be. If you "throw" the ball from around shoulder height or below, as many club players tend to do, your toss—and your serve—will be erratic. The ball should be in the air for as short a time as possible.

6 **Open your fingers to let go of the ball.** As you bring the ball up, you should hold it in your fingertips with just enough pressure to keep the ball in position until you release it. At the top of your reach, all you have to do is open your fingers and the ball will continue on its upward path. If you are holding the ball properly, the opening of your fingers will be almost imperceptible and the ball will leave your hand without spinning. (Incidentally, I don't think you can hold two balls and toss the first ball correctly. So put the second ball in your pocket until you actually need it.) After you release the ball, let your arm continue upward into a kind of follow-through. That will help give you a smooth, relaxed motion.

7 **Toss the ball to your highest reach.** I see many club players who toss the ball too high or too low. How far should the ball travel? Just as high as you can reach with your racquet. If you toss the ball higher than that, it will be falling as you hit it and, thus, present you with a harder target to hit. If you toss the ball too low, you'll have a cramped swing which will have little power. In both cases, your arm motion won't be synchronized with the ball toss and that means the serve will not be smooth and rhythmic. The ball doesn't have to rise more than three feet or so after leaving your hand. And three feet is a short enough distance for you to be able to deliver the ball to the same place time after time. Like everything else in tennis, though, the ball toss needs practice.

8 **Follow the ball as you toss it.** The ball shouldn't rise straight above you as you make your toss. You should toss it slightly in front of you and to your right (if you are a right-hander) so that you can move forward into it with your racquet. Tossed properly, the ball should fall into the court about a racquet's length in front of the baseline. The exact distance will vary, depending on your serve. If you lean heavily as you serve, like Roscoe Tanner, you should toss a little farther into the court. But if you toss the ball so close to you that it would hit you on the head if it came down, you won't be able to lean into your serve at all. Toss the ball forward and to the right slightly and follow it with your body so you can put weight into your serve.

9 **Toss the ball right to serve right.** You may be thinking I've given you a lot of points to keep in mind about an action that you thought was pretty simple. But you'll never learn to serve well until you get the ball toss down properly. So there are three important points that I'd like to re-emphasize: hold the ball in your fingertips; release the ball at the top of your reach; and make sure your weight is moving forward as you start your ball toss. If you can keep just those three things in mind, you'll be well on the way to developing the consistent ball toss that will put new authority in your serve.

7 HOW TO HIT A SLICE SERVE

1 **Why it's the best serve.** If you've been playing tennis for any length of time, you'll have heard about all the different types of serves—flat, spin, twist, kick and so on. Well, forget them. What most club players need is one good, solid, reliable serve that lets them get the ball in with something on it, day in and day out, match after match. The serve that best does that for you is the slice. So it's the one I recommend you practice and perfect.

A slice serve is nothing more than a serve hit with spin. The spin makes the ball curve through the air before and after the bounce, meaning the ball's tougher to return. It also pulls the ball down into the service box, helping you to get more deliveries in. If you can learn how to slice your serve, you can quit worrying about that part of your game. It will become as dependable as your old forehand. And you can concentrate on more important matters—playing, winning and enjoying your matches.

2 **Use a backhand grip.** There's nothing terribly difficult about hitting the slice serve. The first step is to hold your racquet with a backhand grip (see the drawing on the left). That puts your racquet head in position to brush the back of the ball at contact and put the spin on your serve. The backhand grip may seem a little awkward at first, and you may spray your early attempts to the left of the service box (if you're right-handed). But keep at it. If you have trouble with the backhand grip, try edging toward that side gradually over a period of a few weeks.

4 **Get your racquet all the way back.** The second key to getting power into your slice serve is to take your racquet back as far as possible so that you can swing at the ball with a big circular motion. The bigger this circular motion, the more you'll be able to accelerate the racquet head as you bring it up to meet the ball. Let the racquet head drop back behind you so that your elbow is up in the air (see the drawing on the right) and your wrist is cocked back. This position is usually called "backscratching," but there's no need to have the racquet head actually hit your back. Let the head swing back and down with the same fluid motion you'd use to throw your jacket casually over your shoulders.

3 **Move your weight into the ball.** Besides spin, you also need power to put some authority in your slice serve. To get that, you have to throw your weight into your serve, a movement that begins with the ball toss (see my article in the December issue). Your racquet first comes up and behind you on the backswing. Then, as you swing up to hit the ball, keep your body moving forward by swinging your hips toward the court. The action is like the one that a golfer uses as he prepares to drive the ball. Let your hips flow forward so that your weight is mainly on your front foot. But keep your racquet-arm shoulder back until you start your forward swing. This swaying motion is like that of a slow disco number. If you move well on the dance floor, you ought to be able to swing your weight into your serve, too.

5 **Swing up to hit the ball.** Until you complete your back-swing, your serve should be a relatively slow motion. But now, on the forward swing, you must speed things up. The idea is to get the head of your racquet moving as fast as possible at the point where you make contact with the ball. That will put power and, oddly enough, more spin on your serve since the harder you hit the ball the more spin you'll get on it (provided you're using the backhand grip). Swing up to the ball as though you were trying to throw your racquet over the net. Your wrist should be relatively loose as you start the swing and become firmer as you approach the point of contact. As you can see from the drawing on the left, my racquet moves through a bigger arc than my arm. So there has to be some wrist movement to let the racquet head accelerate to its top speed. Use a throwing action and you'll soon get the feel for this acceleration of the racquet head.

6 **Brush the ball.** To make the ball spin, the strings must brush it with a sideways motion as contact is made. If your service motion is correct and you're using a backhand grip, this brushing action will come quite naturally. Bring your racquet head up over your hitting shoulder and not directly over your head. If you have to bring the racquet over your head, you've placed the ball in the wrong spot on your ball toss. When you make contact (see the drawing on the left), your arm should move slightly outward as you swing through the ball. At the same time, your backhand grip will cause the racquet head to move around the ball (see the drawing on the right). These two movements will add sidespin, or slice, to your serve. Don't try to overemphasize the slicing action as you hit. Remember to hit through the ball (in order to make the ball go deep in your opponent's court) and let your grip and arm motion apply the spin naturally. You can use this serve for both your first and second serves but you'll get so many first serves in that you'll rarely hit a second.

7 **Lean into your hit.** When you make contact with the ball, you should be almost falling into the court in order to put everything you've got into your delivery. I actually jump into the air as I serve; in fact, there's a straight line from my back foot to the tip of my racquet at contact. Jumping into the serve isn't for everybody, I'll admit, so if you can't do it, don't worry. However, you should lean forward into the serve as you hit so that you are forced to take one step into the court as you complete your serve. By doing that, you'll be sure to keep your weight moving forward throughout your serve. If you think of your arm as the small hand of a clock, you should hit the ball at the 1:30 position (10:30 for left-handers), out in front and to the side.

8 **Snap your wrist for added power.** If you hit your serve with the throwing action I recommend, you will find that you'll move the racquet head faster by snapping your wrist through ball contact. Most tennis strokes, of course, should be hit with a firm wrist. But the serve needs that wrist motion to add extra power to the stroke. At contact you should be snapping your wrist forward and then continue the snap to the follow-through (as I'm doing in the drawing on the right). But you must make contact with the ball in front of you. You don't need brute force for a powerful serve—it's more a matter of putting all the pieces together at the right time. And the wrist snap is one of the important components of a good serve.

9 **Finish your follow-through.** The serve doesn't stop when you've hit the ball. Let the racquet head flow into the follow-through in as big an arc as possible. If you stop your follow-through prematurely, the chances are that your racquet head will be slowing down as you hit the ball. That means you won't be getting the maximum power and you'll be wasting much of the effort that you put into your backswing. So really hurl yourself into the serve with a big sweep of your racquet into the follow-through. Your racquet arm should swing across your body so that the racquet head ends up pointing behind you on the opposite side from where you hit the ball. Check yourself occasionally in practice by stopping after you've served and note the position of your racquet head. If it's behind you, your follow-through was good.

J McQueen

10 **Follow your serve to the net.** If you lean into the serve properly, you'll have to take at least one full step into the court to regain your balance. At that point, you can retreat a few steps if you want to play the point from the baseline. That's usually sensible on a slow surface. Otherwise, though, you have a fine opportunity to seize the initiative by moving toward the net behind the ball. In fact, a slice serve does two things to help you play a serve-and-volley game. First, the arc that the spin puts on the ball will give you enough time to get up to the service line for your first volley. Second, a sliced ball presents a tough target for the receiver and, thus, reduces the chances that he or she will hit a good return. One of the dividends of the slice serve is that you can use it for both your first and second serves. But once you get the hang of it, you'll probably get so many first serves in that you won't have to resort to a second serve all that often.

8 HOW TO HIT BETTER RETURNS

1 A critical shot. Once you advance beyond the beginner level, your return of serve becomes a vitally important shot. In singles, in order to win any match, you have to break your opponent's serve at least once (unless you go into a tiebreaker). And you can do that only if you have a good return of serve. In fact, a serving team in doubles will demolish you unless you can return low to the server and, thus, force him to hit a tough first volley or a half volley. It is no accident that great champions, all the way from Bill Tilden to Don Budge to Jimmy Connors today, have had great returns of serve. It is a critical shot for you, too.

2 Keep your eyes on the ball. When you are in the ready position, waiting to receive serve, watch the ball rather than the server. After all, the ball is what you are going to hit. So focus on it from the moment the server puts it in his hand. That will help orient your mind to the task ahead: sending that ball back over the net. At the same time, get ready to make your move to the ball. Keep your knees bent and your body flexed; make sure your racquet is out in front so you can draw it quickly to either the backhand or forehand side. This preparation should be automatic so you can devote all your attention to the ball the server is going to hit.

3 Get your racquet head moving first. The key to getting into position to hit a good return of serve is to start your move to the ball almost instinctively as soon as it leaves the other player's racquet. Determine whether the ball is coming to your forehand or backhand and take the head of your racquet to that side right away. Your racquet should be comfortably parallel to the ground in the ready position so that you can draw it back quickly and directly. That will start your upper body turning the way it should. Get your feet moving, too. If the ball's on your right side, push off with your left foot, as I'm doing here, to start moving toward the ball.

4 **When to shorten your backswing.** When you're facing a player with a potent first serve that bounces deep and has some pace on it, you won't have enough time to move into position and get your racquet all the way back. In fact, you won't need the long backswing of an ordinary ground stroke because you can use the pace of the serve itself to send the ball zipping back over the net. Just shorten your backswing a little so you can swing forward and meet the ball slightly in front of you. The bigger the backswing you take at a hard serve, the bigger the hole you'll dig for yourself because you won't have the time to swing forward and hit the ball correctly.

5 **Block a cannonball serve.** If you are up against someone with a smoking cannonball serve, be content just to block the ball back. Take a very short backswing and block the ball using a firm wrist and grip. Do no more than attempt to guide the ball back over the net. It's almost a matter of simply letting the ball hit the racquet although, of course, you must have some forward swing in order to control the ball. Don't try any fancy placements; just go for a firm crosscourt return. Remember, when you are facing a player with a bullet serve, your sole objective should be to get the ball back over the net. In fact, that can often be enough; the server may be so proud of his delivery that you'll catch him off-guard with your return!

6 **Use a chip for error-free returns.** As your game improves, I suggest that you begin to develop a chip return of serve; that is, a return hit with some underspin. Underspin will make the ball rise slightly so that it has a better chance of clearing the net. It will also let you hit the ball deep against a server who stays back, or shorter to the feet of a net-rushing server. To chip your returns, simply take the racquet back a little higher than usual and hit through the ball on a slightly downward plane with a racquet face that's tilted back just a fraction. This motion will put underspin on the ball and let you hit through it properly for depth.

7 **Stay down for a solid return.** There should be no wasted motion on your return of serve; no bobbing up and down in the ready position or during the swing. In fact, you should bend your knees and stay in the same horizontal plane through your forward swing, as I'm doing here. If there were a board over my head at the start of the swing, I wouldn't rise any higher until my return of serve was completed. If you stay down, you'll be able to put your weight into the shot and, as a result, hit a more powerful return. Besides, your eyes will be nearer to the ball, which will permit you to aim your return more accurately. The closer you keep your eyes to the ball, the better off you'll be. So stay down throughout the stroke, right into the follow-through.

8 **Pick your shot before you hit.** One of the most common mistakes club players make is to change their minds about where they're going to hit the ball while they're swinging at it. So decide what you're going to do with each return of serve before the ball is hit to you. The decision is usually quite simple but, once made, you should stick to it. The safest return of serve is crosscourt, deep to the opposite corner. You'll have more room for error if you go that way. A down-the-line shot is not only tougher, but you'll also have less margin for error because the net is higher. If you are facing a player who always follows his first serve to the net, you should still return crosscourt; just hit a shot that's more shallow so the server has to hit a low volley from near his feet.

9 **Try to take the ball on the rise.** To get the maximum advantage from your return of serve, you should hit the ball as early as you can—or, as they sometimes say, take it on the rise. That means making contact with the ball before it reaches the top of its bounce. You'll give the server less time to react to your return or to get into a good position for a first volley if he's a net-rusher. You'll notice that an aggressive player like Jimmy Connors (above) often moves in on a serve, takes the ball early and hits such a powerful return that he gets a winner or forces an error. Try that tactic for yourself, especially when your opponent hits a second serve. Move in a few feet for the return and take it on the rise. You'll now be on the offensive and on your way toward winning the point. Of course, you have to be quick to hit the ball early. And timing is the key. The secret to acquiring that lies, as mastery of anything on court does, in practice. So start out by taking slower serves on the rise and then move in on progressively faster ones as your timing improves.

PART II
PLAYING AT NET

9 MASTERING THE FOREHAND VOLLEY

1 **Keep it short and simple.** On the face of it, a volley is a very simple stroke. All that's involved, basically, is taking a quick punch at the ball before it bounces. There's more to it than that, as we'll see, especially since a volley is hit when you're up near the net where the ball comes at you faster than it does back at the baseline. For that reason, you don't have the luxury of taking a long backswing as you do on ground strokes. If you do, the chances are you'll swing too late to meet the ball solidly. So the volley is a short, quick stroke that you should execute almost instinctively. The main thing is to keep the stroke simple so that you don't have to think about it when you're involved in some fast-paced action at the net. Many weekend players have poor volleys because they rarely practice the shot. You'll have to work on your volleys to keep them short and simple.

2 **Use one grip at the net.** Because the pace of play at the net is so fast, most good players prefer to use one grip to hit both forehand and backhand volleys. So they often have a grip that is between the Eastern forehand and backhand grips (see far left)—sometimes called a "Continental" grip since it was originally favored by many European players. However, I recommend that novice players use a proper forehand grip (see near left) and change their grip for the backhand volley. Later, when your volleys improve, you can gradually alter your grip so that you eventually end up with one grip for all your volleys. As you modify your grip, the "V" formed by your thumb and first finger should gradually move to the center of the top panel of the racquet handle (see far left). You can use this grip for both volleys.

3 **Wait with your racquet up.** You should keep your racquet head high when you are playing at the net. The tip of your racquet head should be just below eye level so that you can move the racquet quickly to either side to intercept the ball. It's important to keep your racquet up because most of the balls that you have to volley will be at net height or higher. Use your other hand to steady the racquet and to guide the head as you prepare to volley. Keep your weight forward on the balls of your feet so that you can step out quickly to reach for wide balls. And, of course, your eyes should be glued to the ball that your opponent is hitting.

4 **Turn the racquet.** Because time is short at the net, you should use little or no backswing when hitting a volley. In fact, I hesitate to employ the word "backswing" in connection with the volley because I prefer that beginners use virtually none at all on the shot. From the ready position, all you need do is turn the head of the racquet so that the strings face the ball. Then, simply meet the ball out in front of you. As your volleying improves, you can take a short backswing by turning your shoulders and opening the face of the racquet with the racquet still held high. You should not let the racquet go further back than your shoulder (see left). If you find that you are mis-timing your volleys, shorten your swing again until you are meeting the ball squarely.

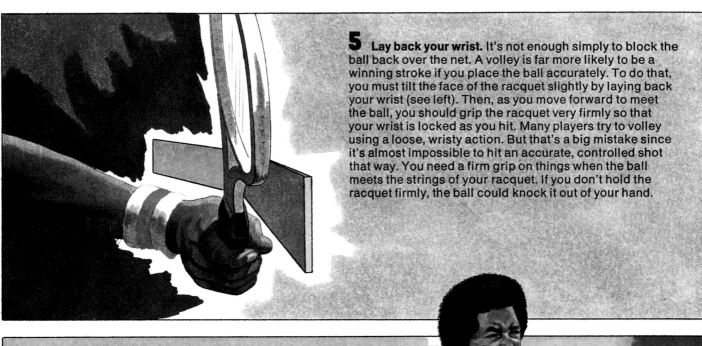

5 **Lay back your wrist.** It's not enough simply to block the ball back over the net. A volley is far more likely to be a winning stroke if you place the ball accurately. To do that, you must tilt the face of the racquet slightly by laying back your wrist (see left). Then, as you move forward to meet the ball, you should grip the racquet very firmly so that your wrist is locked as you hit. Many players try to volley using a loose, wristy action. But that's a big mistake since it's almost impossible to hit an accurate, controlled shot that way. You need a firm grip on things when the ball meets the strings of your racquet. If you don't hold the racquet firmly, the ball could knock it out of your hand.

6 **Step toward the ball.** Whenever you have enough time, you should move toward the ball as you hit your forehand volleys. Being in the right place is half the game when you're volleying. If you can't get to the ball, then you can't hit it. Take short, rapid steps to get close to the ball and make your final step with the foot farthest away from the ball (see inset above). If you're a right-hander, that means pivoting on your right foot, and stepping toward the ball with your left foot. This last step will allow you to stretch out for the ball if you've misjudged its flight. You will also be moving your weight into the shot, which will give you a little extra power. But, more importantly, you will be properly balanced and ready to recover for your next shot.

7 **Hit the ball out in front.** You should try to meet the ball well out in front of you. That's because you can see the ball better when it's in front and can angle the ball more sharply if necessary. Don't worry that you'll sacrifice power by hitting the ball way out in front. Almost all the power you'll need is supplied by the pace of your opponent's shot. Ken Rosewall has never volleyed the ball hard in his life, but his volleys are crisp and placed exactly where he wants them to go. As you hit your volley, your elbow and forearm should be moving forward together. Don't swing your arm around your body—keep everything moving forward into the ball. You can angle your volleys by opening or closing your racquet face a little (that is, tilting it back or forward slightly). But don't tilt it too much or you'll be hitting with a weak wrist. Just open the racquet face a little more to send the ball down the line or close it slightly to angle the ball crosscourt.

8 **Use a brief follow-through.** The punching action of the forehand volley should be completed with a relatively short follow-through. Simply let the racquet head continue after the ball in the direction you wish to send it. A short follow-through will help you place the ball accurately and a long follow-through won't add anything to your shot. In fact, all it will do is slow your preparation for your next shot. That's a particular handicap in doubles at those times when all four players are stationed up close to the net banging away at the ball. If you use a long follow-through, you'll restrict your chances of hitting another volley properly. So keep your follow-through short—but not so short that the ball merely pops weakly off your racquet.

J McQueen

1 **Keep it simple.** The backhand volley is one of the easiest of tennis shots to hit —provided that you keep things simple. There's almost nothing to the shot because the backswing is very short and the forward swing is just a swift, punching motion without a long follow-through. The problem, of course, is that you have very little time at the net to get into position to make a precise and well-controlled shot. The ball is coming at you so fast you have to hit it instinctively. That means your volleys should be grooved through lots of practice so you never have to think about them during your matches. If your volley goes sour when you play, simplify it—cut down on the backswing and shorten your forward swing. Most of the volleying errors made by club players are caused by trying to do too much with a stroke that should be kept simple.

2 **Use one grip for all your volleys.** When you first practice your forehand and backhand volleys, you'll be able to hit the ball more easily if you use the Eastern forehand and backhand grips (below). However, in actual play, you'll find that there just isn't enough time— especially in doubles—to change your grip between the forehand and backhand sides. So you should try to use an in-between grip, the Continental, for all your volleys. The Continental grip puts the "V"—at the junction of your thumb and palm—almost in the center of the top panel of your racquet handle. You may find the Continental a little awkward at first, but using one grip will help you react faster.

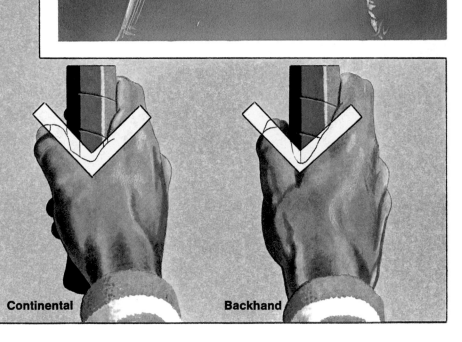

Forehand   Continental   Backhand

3 **Hold your racquet up in front.**
When you're playing at the net, you should keep your racquet up in front of you. That's because most balls will come to you at about chest height and all you'll need to do is swing the racquet head to the side in order to prepare for your volley. If you let the racquet head droop, you'll waste valuable time and effort bringing the head up to the level of the ball's flight. You'll also save time by waiting with your racquet exactly in front of you so that the head has to move an equal distance for a forehand or backhand volley.

4 **Use your other hand to guide the racquet.**
One plus you have with the backhand volley is that you can easily use your other hand to brace your racquet as you make your short backswing. Your other hand can act as a guide and a brake to make sure that you don't take the racquet too far back. Preparing for the volley is almost like setting up with a catapult in your racquet hand. Turn your upper body if you have time so that you can uncoil on the forward swing to get more power behind the shot.

5 **Watch the ball closely.** I can never emphasize too much the importance of keeping your eyes on the ball—especially when you're at the net. You have so little time to react when volleying that you can't afford the slightest lapse of concentration. I have a little trick that I use to aid my own concentration. When my opponent hits the ball, I inhale sharply and then breathe out as I hit my volley. I don't quite know why, but holding my breath this way helps me focus on the ball even more keenly. But it's probably the same principle that's at work in karate where competitors will exhale loudly as they deliver their blows. Whatever the reason, the technique works for me—and maybe it will for you, too.

6 **Move in to meet the ball.** As you make contact with the ball, you should be moving forward in order to put a little weight into the shot and to hit the ball aggressively. Even though you employ a short forward swing on the backhand volley, you'll get plenty of power into the shot if you use your body weight and keep a firm wrist and grip. I prefer to hit my volleys with a slightly open racquet face (right); that way, I add a little underspin so I can control the direction and depth of my volleys. The underspin makes the ball stay low, which means my opponent will have to hit up if he manages to return my volley. Remember that the volley should be a winning stroke when you are close to the net. So go for the ball aggressively by moving forward to meet it.

7 **Limit your follow-through.** It's a great feeling when you snap off a crisp backhand volley. But don't get carried away. You will be opening up your body as you hit, so it's tempting to let the racquet sail into an extravagantly long follow-through. Resist that temptation. All you need is a short follow-through to complete the punching motion of this stroke. Let the racquet follow the ball's direction briefly and then bring it back quickly to get into the ready position for your next shot. A long follow-through will add nothing to your shot and will only delay your recovery. Keep the stroke short and simple.

8 **Handling a low backhand volley.** When you follow your serve to the net, you'll often have to hit a low first volley from close to the service line. That's the toughest volley to cope with because you're in a hurry to get to the net and you'll have to hit the ball up to get it back over the net. Don't try anything fancy. Pause briefly as the ball approaches, bend your knees and upper body to get down to the ball, and hit it firmly without letting the racquet head drop too far. If you do that, you'll probably hit a weak, uncontrolled shot. Send the ball crosscourt because it will cross the middle of the net where it's lowest and because you'll have more court to aim at with your shot. Go for a sound, conservative stroke and then move in closer to the net for your next volley—which should be higher if your first volley was successful.

9 **Returning a ball hit right at you.** Sometimes, particularly in doubles when everybody is up at the net, you'll have to deal with a ball that's aimed directly at you. You will rarely have time to get out of the way and hit an orthodox volley. The best response is to use your backhand volley, both to defend yourself and to get the ball back. Your backhand volley can cover almost all of your upper body, while you'd have to move out of the way of the ball to hit a decent forehand volley. You can still hit a respectable backhand volley since you'll have room to make a short punching stroke. On occasion, though, it's enough simply to hold the racquet firmly and block the ball back, using the pace that's already on it. As with the low volley, your main concern should be to get the ball back over the net.

1 **Make your smash a winner.** The overhead smash is not an easy shot. It takes coordination, timing and practice to master. But it's worth the effort because, done right, it will often be a winner. The reason many club players have trouble with the overhead is that they whale away at the ball trying to blast it past an opponent—which is why they often suffer the embarrassment of a complete miss or a wild mis-hit. Instead, like the serve, the overhead should be a controlled shot—hit carefully and placed properly. In fact, if you can serve adequately, you can also develop a reliable overhead. In the following panels, I'll show you how to do it.

2 **How to hold your racquet.** Since the overhead is much like the serve, you should use the same grip that you use to serve. I prefer the backhand grip because that lets me put enough spin on the ball for good control; but if you use a modified backhand grip like the Continental, that's fine, too. I use an Eastern backhand grip with the hand rotated about a quarter of a turn over the top of the racquet from the standard Eastern forehand "shake-hands" grip. As in the drawing (right), the "V" between your thumb and index finger should be directly over the edge formed by the top of the racquet handle and the left-hand bevel (right-hand bevel for left-handers).

3 **Be ready to move fast.** Most of your overhead opportunities will come when you're playing at the net and your opponent sends up a lob attempting to drive you into the backcourt. You won't know until your opponent has hit the ball whether you are going to have to hit a volley or move back for a smash. So you should be prepared for either. Stand with your weight forward slightly, poised on the balls of your feet, and with your racquet head held well up in front of you— as I'm doing on the left. In this stance, you'll be set to take the racquet back quickly for a volley or the start of a smash.

4 **Get sideways to the ball.** Your very first movement when you realize that you are going to have to hit an overhead should be to raise your racquet hand up to shoulder level and turn sideways to the flight of the ball. That shoulder turn will get your racquet moving back and let you bring your other hand up to start tracking the ball. If the lob is short, that may be all that you'll have time to do before swinging at the ball (see panel No. 7). The chances are, however, that you'll have to move back to get in the right position to meet the ball.

5 **Skip back on your toes.** Good footwork is essential on the overhead. As you're preparing your racquet for the shot, you'll probably have to retreat at least several steps and adjust your lateral position at the same time. Use short, sideways skipping steps. That permits you to move backward, yet still keep your center of gravity forward. And stay on your toes. You sometimes see players fall down on overheads, and the reason they lose their balance is that they're moving backward with their weight on their heels. If you skip back on your toes, it will help you keep properly balanced.

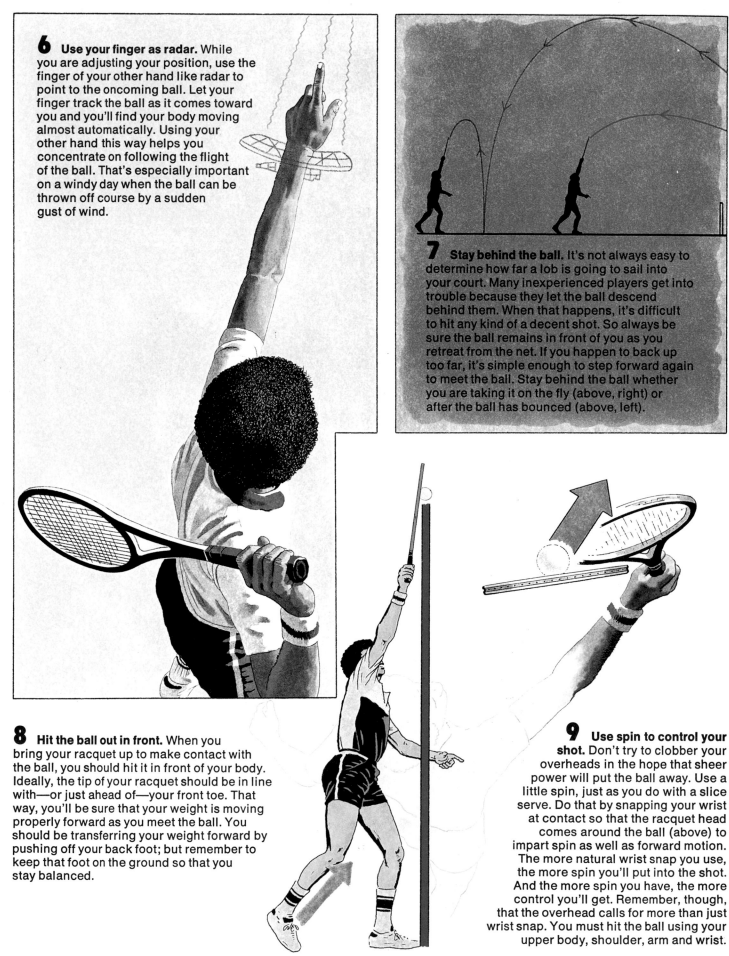

6 **Use your finger as radar.** While you are adjusting your position, use the finger of your other hand like radar to point to the oncoming ball. Let your finger track the ball as it comes toward you and you'll find your body moving almost automatically. Using your other hand this way helps you concentrate on following the flight of the ball. That's especially important on a windy day when the ball can be thrown off course by a sudden gust of wind.

7 **Stay behind the ball.** It's not always easy to determine how far a lob is going to sail into your court. Many inexperienced players get into trouble because they let the ball descend behind them. When that happens, it's difficult to hit any kind of a decent shot. So always be sure the ball remains in front of you as you retreat from the net. If you happen to back up too far, it's simple enough to step forward again to meet the ball. Stay behind the ball whether you are taking it on the fly (above, right) or after the ball has bounced (above, left).

8 **Hit the ball out in front.** When you bring your racquet up to make contact with the ball, you should hit it in front of your body. Ideally, the tip of your racquet should be in line with—or just ahead of—your front toe. That way, you'll be sure that your weight is moving properly forward as you meet the ball. You should be transferring your weight forward by pushing off your back foot; but remember to keep that foot on the ground so that you stay balanced.

9 **Use spin to control your shot.** Don't try to clobber your overheads in the hope that sheer power will put the ball away. Use a little spin, just as you do with a slice serve. Do that by snapping your wrist at contact so that the racquet head comes around the ball (above) to impart spin as well as forward motion. The more natural wrist snap you use, the more spin you'll put into the shot. And the more spin you have, the more control you'll get. Remember, though, that the overhead calls for more than just wrist snap. You must hit the ball using your upper body, shoulder, arm and wrist.

10 **Jump only when you must.**
Always try to take your overheads
with both feet planted on the
court. That gives you a solid,
balanced base for the stroke, and
you'll also be able to recover
rapidly for your next shot. But
there are occasions when an
opponent tosses up a quick
offensive lob that's so good you
have little or no time to retreat.
You have to leap for it if you hope
to get the ball back. In that case,
jump off the leg on your racquet
side—pushing off so that you
get the same swing and body
movement that you would use for
a standing overhead. Try to time
the jump so that you are still able
to hit the ball out in front of you.
Of course, the jumping overhead
is a desperation shot, so the big
thing is simply to make sure you
get the ball back and prevent it
from looping over you for a
probable winner.

J. McQueen

11 **Recover fast and be ready.** After you've hit an
overhead, recover promptly and scamper back to the
net. (When you've had to hit your smash from deep in
your court, however, take up a position back on the
baseline.) If you've had to jump for the ball, you're apt
to be vulnerable as you land on the court; you may be
off balance and not fully prepared to react to your
opponent's return. So come down on your toes and
bounce lightly—like a gymnast finishing his routine.
Whether you jump or not, remember that your
opponent's reply is likely to be a weak shot. So be
ready to move in and put the ball away.

PART III
ADVANCED SHOTMAKING

12 HOW TO WIN WITH SPIN

1 Add an extra dimension. There's a lot of emphasis in the pro game today on using spin, especially topspin, because it's such a strong feature of the games of such stars as Bjorn Borg and Guillermo Vilas. Of course, there's nothing new about using spin. In fact, the definitive book on the subject is Bill Tilden's "Match Play and the Spin of the Ball," written more than 50 years ago. And, there's no question that spin is an essential part of the better player's game.

However, I hate to see players attempting to use spin before they have mastered at least the basics of sound stroking. When you have a moderately competent serve, reliable ground strokes and can hit passable volleys, then you can think about adding the extra dimension of spin to your game. Spin will give variety to your strokes and boost your confidence in controlling the ball. But, as we'll see, you must use the right kind of spin at the proper time and place.

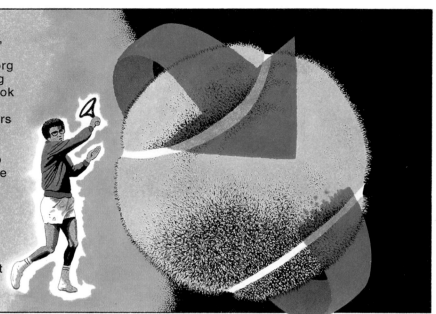

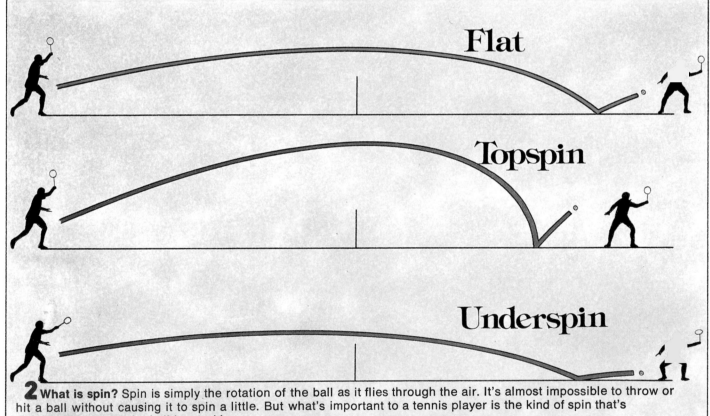

Flat

Topspin

Underspin

2 What is spin? Spin is simply the rotation of the ball as it flies through the air. It's almost impossible to throw or hit a ball without causing it to spin a little. But what's important to a tennis player is the kind of spin that's deliberately put on the ball by stroking.

Most beginners hit the ball flat with little or no spin (top) so that the ball travels through the air in a smooth arc as though it had been shot from a gun. A ball that is hit flat, hard and sufficiently high over the net, can go well beyond the baseline.

A ball hit with topspin—meaning the ball rotates away from the hitter—will drop more sharply and bounce higher (middle) than a flat ball. Hard hitters like Borg and Vilas use topspin to make sure the ball drops well inside the baseline yet bounces high enough to provide a difficult target for the receiver.

By contrast, a ball hit with underspin (bottom), so the underside of the ball rotates away from the hitter, tends to come down slowly, almost floating through the air. On many surfaces, an underspin ball will skid and, as a result, bounce lower than a ball hit without spin, which may prevent the opponent from attacking.

3 **Start with natural topspin.** When you can hit confident ground strokes, the best way to start experimenting with spin is by trying to hit a topspin forehand. Simply take your racquet back lower than for your usual forehand, bring the racquet up to meet the flight of the ball, hit through the ball and finish with a higher than normal follow-through. This low-to-high action will cause you to brush the back of the ball as you hit and will automatically put a natural topspin on the ball.

The amount of topspin will depend on how hard you hit the ball and how rapidly your racquet is moving at contact. Start by making small adjustments in your usual stroke and see how the topspin affects the flight of the ball. You'll find that the more topspin you apply, the faster the ball will drop after crossing the net. But at the same time, your timing must be more precise to avoid mis-hitting the ball. However, a little natural topspin will give your ground strokes that extra margin of safety; they'll be far less likely to go long.

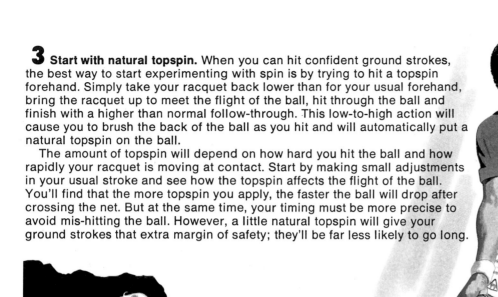

4 **Change your grip for extra topspin.** If you really want to employ the excessive topspin of a Borg or Vilas on your forehand, you'll have to change to a Western grip (see left). To get this grip, lay your racquet on a table and pick it up as though you were taking up a hammer to hit a nail! That will put the fleshy part of your palm almost under the handle as you hit the ball and will enable you to make contact with an upward whipping action like Borg (far left) does. But I must caution you that this stroke is tough on your wrist and elbow, and requires incredibly precise timing.

5 **Put some slice into your backhand.** The shot where you can probably use spin most safely and effectively is the backhand. In fact, I think your bread-and-butter backhand should be the slice or underspin shot. It needs less effort than a topspin shot and the ball's pace and depth can be controlled. The motion involved in slicing your backhand is the reverse of the natural topspin forehand: take your racquet back shoulder high, come down to meet the ball and follow through out in front of you. If your racquet head is moving down as you hit the ball, you'll brush the back of it and that will put underspin on it. An underspin shot will tend to go lower over the net, but a softly hit shot will float and go deep.

6 **Use underspin to control your low volleys.** The advantages of depth and control that underspin brings to a backhand ground stroke can also be applied to your volleys—especially those troublesome low volleys. Many club players simply scoop low volleys back over the net where they can easily be picked off by an aggressive opponent. To prevent that, hit your volleys with a high-to-low stroking action (left), swinging firmly through the ball at the same time.

7 **Hit your approach shots with sidespin.** An approach shot should keep your opponent back so he can't hit an effective passing shot as you continue to move up to the net. You can make your approach shots even tougher to return by adding sidespin with what I call the "inside-out" shot. It's easiest to do that on the backhand side. Start your forward swing with your racquet fairly high and well away from your body. Bring the racquet head down toward your body as you hit, following through out after the ball.
This movement of the racquet head across the line of flight of the ball will add sidespin and underspin—producing a ball that will go deep and curve away from your opponent.

8 **Try topspin to put bite into your lobs.** Topspin can be a lethal weapon when you want to hit an offensive lob. You have to pick the right ball, of course, because you must swing hard and fast both to hit up and put topspin on at the same time. You can do that only with a ball that's between waist and shoulder high.
But have you ever thought of using topspin on your defensive lobs, too? I know the defensive lob is a shot that's often used as a last-ditch effort to stay in the point when you're deep in the court. But there are occasions when you may deliberately choose to hit a lob from the baseline area. When you do, try adding some topspin, just as I suggested you do with your normal forehand ground stroke. That way, you can turn the lob into more of an attacking shot, keeping it lower but still deep, of course. With enough topspin, the ball will kick away after bouncing and may well be unreturnable. So you may turn a defensive lob into a winning shot.

9 **How to defend against spin.** When you face experienced opponents, you can expect that they will be using spin against you. Hitting a heavily spinning ball is not as easy as returning a flat ball. If you ignore the spin, chances are you'll hit underspin balls into the net and pop topspin balls into the air. The answer? Return spin with spin. Watch how your opponent hits his ball. For example, if the racquet head goes from low to high, expect a topspin shot. And prepare to return it with underspin of your own by taking your racquet back high and coming down to meet the ball squarely. What you will be doing is adding to your opponent's spin. If your opponent's racquet goes from high to low expect an underspin ball and prepare with your racquet low.

10 **Make spin work for you.** Because some of the top playing professionals have games that are heavily dependent on spin, I see some younger players who try to hit every shot with spin. That's a mistake, I think. You should use spin to give variety to your strokes, to add control and to keep your opponent guessing. If you hit every ball with topspin your opponent knows exactly what to expect and can react faster. On the other hand, if you mix up your shots, you'll give your opponent less time to decide how to reply.

Watch John McEnroe (right) play. He has such great racquet-head control, of course, that he can put the ball exactly where he wants. But he never uses too much spin; just the amount that's necessary. That's what you should aim for with spin. Experiment a little, find out what suits your style of play and employ it when necessary. Sure it's fun to hit heavy underspin drop shots that climb back over the net. But how many times do they work? Use spin to increase your chances of winning, not your chances of making an error.

13 HOW TO HIT AN APPROACH SHOT

1 What it is. The approach shot is an indispensable tool for the aggressive player who plays best at the net. Quite simply, the approach shot is any shot you hit in the mid-court area in order to gain (i.e., approach) the net. However, that simplicity ends with the definition because making a good approach shot is quite complicated. While you use either a basic forehand or backhand ground stroke, everything happens at once with the approach shot.

You have to move up inside the baseline to take the ball, which means you can choose only balls that land short. You have to pause for a moment to make your shot, which must be carefully placed to give your opponent little chance of stinging you with a successful passing shot. And the moment the ball leaves your racquet, you have to keep moving up to the net to be in a good position to make your first volley. All that calls for some sharp reactions and good, solid stroking technique.

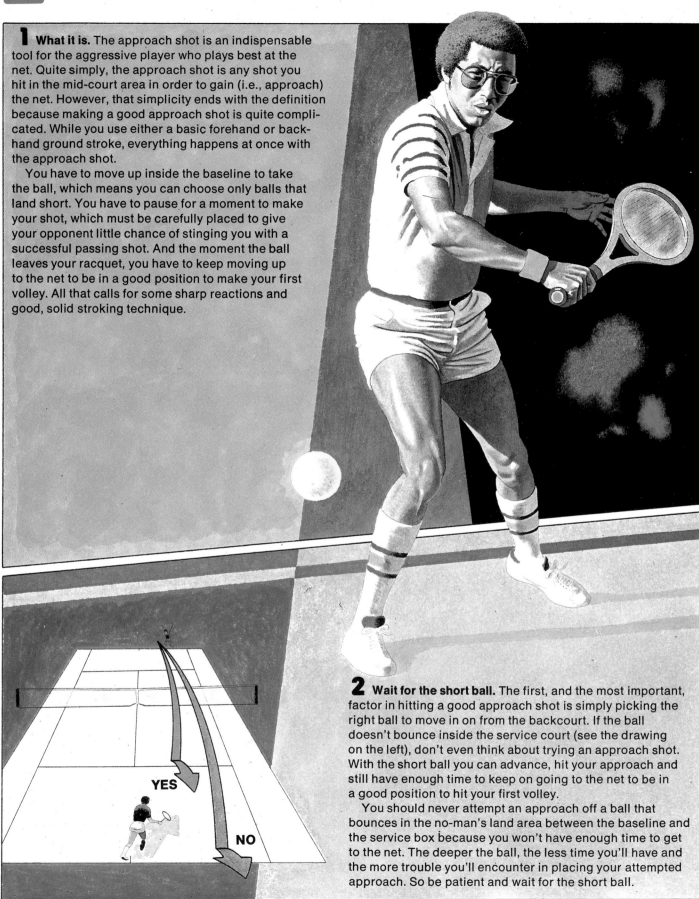

YES

NO

2 Wait for the short ball. The first, and the most important, factor in hitting a good approach shot is simply picking the right ball to move in on from the backcourt. If the ball doesn't bounce inside the service court (see the drawing on the left), don't even think about trying an approach shot. With the short ball you can advance, hit your approach and still have enough time to keep on going to the net to be in a good position to hit your first volley.

You should never attempt an approach off a ball that bounces in the no-man's land area between the baseline and the service box because you won't have enough time to get to the net. The deeper the ball, the less time you'll have and the more trouble you'll encounter in placing your attempted approach. So be patient and wait for the short ball.

3 **Take a shorter backswing.** The fundamentals of the approach shot are pretty much like those of a conventional ground stroke because you want the ball to go deep in your opponent's court so he'll have a hard time trying to pass you at the net. However, the ball must travel a shorter distance than a normal baseline-to-baseline ground stroke. As a result, the approach should be a more compact shot than ordinary ground strokes. You can take a shorter backswing because you don't have to hit the ball as hard. But don't cut your backswing so short that you merely pop the ball back over the net.

4 **Hit the ball out in front.** The name of the game on the approach shot is to control the ball so you can place it accurately. As I see it, the only way to do that is to hit the ball a little farther out in front than you do on a normal ground stroke and to let your body stay with the shot for a bit so you have a smooth, flowing stroke.

One of the reasons Jimmy Connors has had problems with his approach shots is his tendency to hit every ground stroke like a baseball batter. He pivots strongly off his rear foot as he brings his racquet around his body. That's O.K. on a regular ground stroke where you want more of a round-house swing. But it cuts down on the control you need to place an approach shot carefully.

Hitting the ball out in front reduces the chances that your body will pivot like a batter's does and, at the same time, encourages you to swing smoothly through the ball. The forward momentum you generate, moreover, will help you keep going to the net after you hit the ball.

5 **Follow through after the ball.** Although I want you to think of the approach shot as a more compact action than a ground stroke, don't abbreviate your follow-through. For a smooth stroke, you should follow through after the ball—keeping your racquet pointing at the departing ball for as long as possible. This long follow-through will help you hit a more controlled shot and ensure that you aim the ball properly.

A flowing follow-through comes naturally on the backhand side, especially if you put a little underspin on your approach shot (something I definitely recommend). On the forehand side, you may have to force your follow-through to continue after the ball.

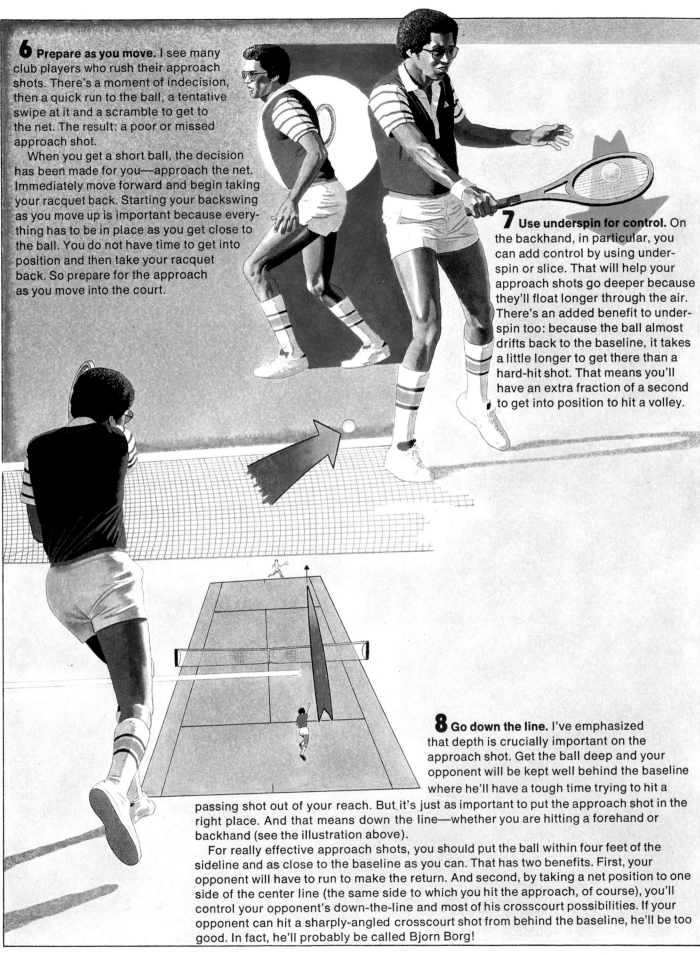

6 **Prepare as you move.** I see many club players who rush their approach shots. There's a moment of indecision, then a quick run to the ball, a tentative swipe at it and a scramble to get to the net. The result: a poor or missed approach shot.

When you get a short ball, the decision has been made for you—approach the net. Immediately move forward and begin taking your racquet back. Starting your backswing as you move up is important because everything has to be in place as you get close to the ball. You do not have time to get into position and then take your racquet back. So prepare for the approach as you move into the court.

7 **Use underspin for control.** On the backhand, in particular, you can add control by using underspin or slice. That will help your approach shots go deeper because they'll float longer through the air. There's an added benefit to underspin too: because the ball almost drifts back to the baseline, it takes a little longer to get there than a hard-hit shot. That means you'll have an extra fraction of a second to get into position to hit a volley.

8 **Go down the line.** I've emphasized that depth is crucially important on the approach shot. Get the ball deep and your opponent will be kept well behind the baseline where he'll have a tough time trying to hit a passing shot out of your reach. But it's just as important to put the approach shot in the right place. And that means down the line—whether you are hitting a forehand or backhand (see the illustration above).

For really effective approach shots, you should put the ball within four feet of the sideline and as close to the baseline as you can. That has two benefits. First, your opponent will have to run to make the return. And second, by taking a net position to one side of the center line (the same side to which you hit the approach, of course), you'll control your opponent's down-the-line and most of his crosscourt possibilities. If your opponent can hit a sharply-angled crosscourt shot from behind the baseline, he'll be too good. In fact, he'll probably be called Bjorn Borg!

9 **Keep moving after you hit the ball.** Don't waste any time after hitting an approach shot. If you come in to hit a short ball, you've already committed yourself to go to the net—irrespective of what happens to your approach shot. If you stop to see what becomes of your approach, you won't have enough time to get into the proper volleying position at the net. So keep moving after you hit the ball.

You will see many pros who do not stop moving forward to hit approach shots. They often make the approach with an open stance, facing the net, and simply keep on going through the shot. I think that's tough for a club player to do, so I'd recommend that you turn sideways as much as possible to make your approach. However, if you have the ability to hit effectively without being turned fully sideways, then do it because that will help you get to the net almost without breaking stride.

10 **Practice your approach shots.** Players with sound ground strokes rarely have trouble with the approach shot. But the approach shot can be a problem for some club players because it is rarely used and practiced even less frequently. In a pro match, an aggressive player, like Vitas Gerulaitis (left), might hit many approach shots whereas the club player will be lucky to hit a couple of dozen even in a long match.

So I suggest you get out and practice some approach shots. Have your practice partner feed you short balls which you run in on from the baseline, hit deep and then move in behind to the net. At first, try to hit every approach shot beyond the baseline. You'll be surprised how hard that is when you're actually trying to do it. Then, reduce the length until your shots start landing inside the baseline. Practice this way and you'll never hit any approach shots into the net. If you have two practice partners, use a two-on-one drill. Start out on your baseline with the other two players stationed at the opposite baseline. Have one of them feed you a short ball, come in to get it, hit an approach shot to the other baseline player who should return it for you to volley and play the point out.

14 HOW TO HIT THE HALF-VOLLEY

1 **When to use it.** The half-volley is something of a compromise shot: it's neither a volley, since it's hit after the ball has just bounced, nor a full-fledged ground stroke, since it involves an abbreviated swing. In fact, the name is a misnomer, too, because the shot is longer than half of a volley. Typically, you'll use the half-volley when you're caught between the baseline and the service line by a ball that bounces almost at your feet. You aren't close enough to hit a volley before the ball bounces, and yet you aren't far enough away from the bounce to hit a regular ground stroke. Instead, you have to use a short stroke that will lift the ball up from your ankle level and send it back smartly over the net. It's a tough shot because you have to hit a half-volley when you are rushed; for example, when you're on your way to the net after serving. You need the half-volley at other times, too, especially in doubles when the other team hits down toward your feet.

2 **Get down to the ball.** When you hit a half-volley, the ball will be close to the ground. So you must get your racquet head down to the ball. That means you have to bend your knees and upper body to get yourself down to a level where you can hit the ball firmly. If you simply drop your racquet head to stroke the ball with a scooping motion, you'll golf a weak shot that, most likely, will go high in the air like a semi-lob. And the chances are that your opponent will be able to put that shot away easily with a smash or high volley. So you must bend your knees to keep your hand and racquet head on roughly the same horizontal plane as you make your stroke. That way, you'll be able to keep a tighter grip on your racquet so you can hit the ball firmly and place it accurately.

3 **Take a short backswing.** There's virtually no backswing with the half-volley. Simply take the racquet to either the forehand or backhand side, tighten your grip, position the racquet handle roughly parallel to the ground and then almost block the ball off the strings. I like to think of the racquet head as being a low wall near the ground. If you take the racquet too far back, your "wall" will be in the wrong place to make contact with the ball. For a good half-volley, you should try to take the ball as soon as you can after the bounce.

4 **Use a firm wrist.** When you prepare to hit a half-volley, you should tighten your grip so you can keep a firm wrist through contact with the ball. Stay down low and hit through the ball with the racquet face tilted back a bit so that the ball will go up and clear the net comfortably. You should make contact with the ball near your front knee and your body should be moving forward to put some extra power into the shot. Don't hit the ball too far in front or you'll end up scooping the ball over the net.

5 **Hitting a backhand half-volley.** Basically, you should use the same technique on the backhand side that you do on the forehand. The stroke requires little or no backswing and you must get down to the ball so you can keep the racquet head up. Many club players, though, have a tendency to hit with a loose wrist on the backhand side. If you keep the handle of the racquet almost parallel to the ground, you'll have a tighter grip and, thus, be able to hold the racquet head steady as you hit the ball. If you let the head drop, you'll risk hitting with a wristy and weak motion. You can't form that wall with your racquet unless you get your wrist down to keep the head up.

6 **Hit down the line.** Give your half-volleys plenty of room for error over the net. Hit the ball up so that it clears the net by one or two feet. As with a ground stroke, you want the ball to go deep to keep your opponent back on the baseline. On both sides I recommend hitting the half-volley down the line. Since you are probably going to continue up to the net after the half-volley, you'll open up less of the court. That's because your opponent will usually return down the line since the crosscourt passing shot will be too difficult. You'll also be in a good position to cut off your opponent's return if you follow your down-the-line shot toward the net. There is one exception, though. If you hit a poor half-volley, you should back up close to your baseline because your opponent is going to move in and hit an attacking shot.

7 **Use a short follow-through.** The follow-through for the half volley is very much like that of a conventional low volley. Let the racquet head follow the ball in the direction you want it to go. The half-volley isn't a powerful stroke, so there's no need for a long, sweeping follow-through. Keep the follow-through short so you can recover quickly and be on your way to the net without a pause in your forward movement. Remember that the forward momentum of your body will carry the ball forward—provided you make contact with a firm wrist and grip. If you pause to hit the ball with a long stroke, you'll probably hit the ball with underspin which, although it will make the ball rise, won't send it deep in your opponent's court. The essence of the half-volley is understatement both on the backswing and the follow-through.

8 **Keep moving after you hit the ball.** Although the half-volley is often a defensive shot that you are forced to use because you haven't had enough time to get in close enough to hit a real volley, don't let that keep you from taking the offensive. After the half-volley, you should continue up toward the net so that your next shot will be a conventional volley. If you've hit a good half-volley, your body momentum will still be moving forward after you've hit the ball. It's a simple matter to keep on moving up to the net. In fact, it's tougher to back up, which you should do only when you've made a poor half-volley that lands short in the other court.

9 **Under pressure, hit the ball firmly.** Even the fastest players, like Vitas Gerulaitis on the right, are often forced to use the half-volley when receivers return balls low to their feet. Although Gerulaitis is obviously in a tight spot here, you can see that his racquet head is up and he's bending low to get to the ball. With his racquet head up and his hand low, he can grip the racquet tightly and keep his wrist firm to hit the ball solidly. You'll also see that he has his eyes fixed on the ball. When you are under pressure and have to half-volley, concentrate on making your racquet present a firm wall to the ball, as Vitas is doing here. Don't worry about your footwork; if you are moving up, your feet will take care of themselves. But do be sure to bend those knees, so that your racquet gets down close to the ground. The sooner you can take the ball after the bounce, the better your half-volley will be— provided you make contact with a firm wrist and grip.

15 HOW TO HIT THE DROP SHOT

1 **A set-up stroke.** Many club players have the mistaken idea that the drop shot is too difficult a stroke for them to use effectively. Their problem is that they have too high expectations for the shot. They expect to win the point outright with it and, frankly, even the pros can't do that consistently. You should think of the drop shot as a set-up stroke—one that will provoke a weak return from your opponent which you can then attack for a probable winner. So your drop shot doesn't have to be textbook perfect. It should be a gentle, but firm stroke that travels relatively low over the net and bounces as short in the other court as possible. If you can put some underspin on the drop shot, so much the better. That will make the ball stand up and give it a little forward movement. Your opponent will have to dash forward and, if he reaches the ball, the odds are that he will make a weak return since he'll have to hit up and over the net from a position quite close to it. If you are prepared, you'll be able to reply with a crisp passing shot or a quick offensive lob that will close out the point in your favor.

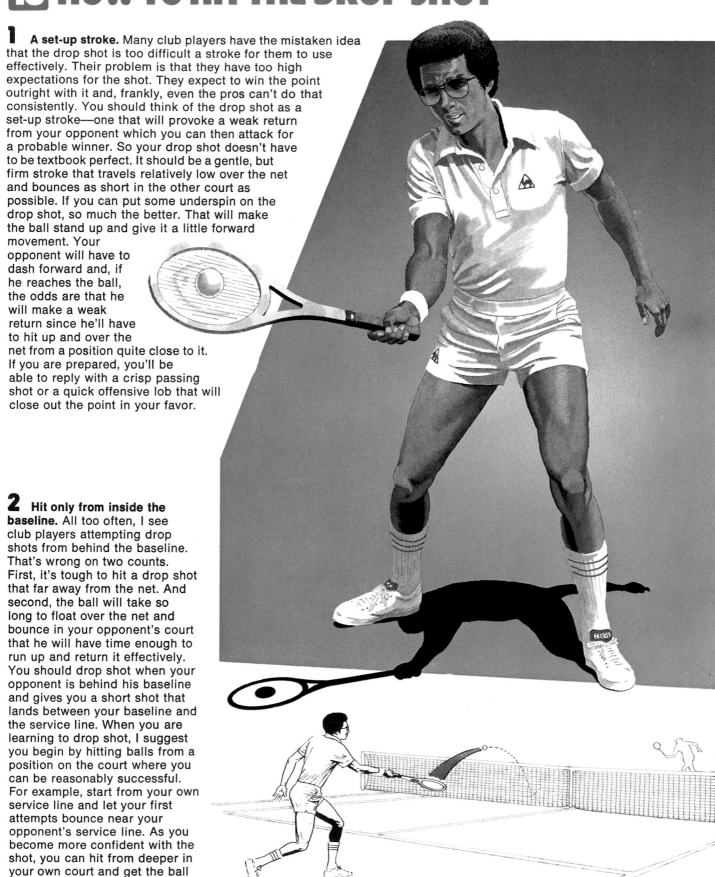

2 **Hit only from inside the baseline.** All too often, I see club players attempting drop shots from behind the baseline. That's wrong on two counts. First, it's tough to hit a drop shot that far away from the net. And second, the ball will take so long to float over the net and bounce in your opponent's court that he will have time enough to run up and return it effectively. You should drop shot when your opponent is behind his baseline and gives you a short shot that lands between your baseline and the service line. When you are learning to drop shot, I suggest you begin by hitting balls from a position on the court where you can be reasonably successful. For example, start from your own service line and let your first attempts bounce near your opponent's service line. As you become more confident with the shot, you can hit from deeper in your own court and get the ball to bounce shorter in your opponent's court.

3 **Prepare as you would for a ground stroke.** When you hit a drop shot, you should disguise the stroke so you don't tip your opponent to what's coming. If he figures that you are about to drop shot, he'll start moving forward in anticipation and that will give him a better chance of handling your shot. So I recommend that you prepare for your drop shots as you would for a normal ground stroke or approach shot. The drop shot is best hit with a little underspin. So take your racquet back as though you were about to hit a sliced backhand or forehand. That means bringing the racquet well back to a fairly high position so you can stroke from high to low to put underspin on the shot. Don't slow your movements down, even though the drop shot is a gentle shot and doesn't really require a full backswing. Anything other than your usual preparation will telegraph the shot to your opponent.

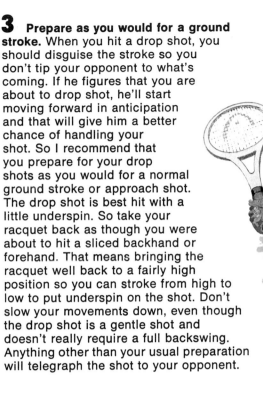

4 **Move toward the ball.** Like your backswing, your forward swing should be identical to the one you'd use if you were about to hit a sliced forehand or backhand. Swing on a downward plane to meet the ball out in front and step toward the ball as you hit. Although weight transfer isn't as important as it is on a normal ground stroke or approach shot, don't forget that you are still trying to disguise this stroke. Only at the last moment before contact should you slow things down and attempt to take the pace off the ball. Keep your wrist firm and move toward the ball as you would for a ground stroke.

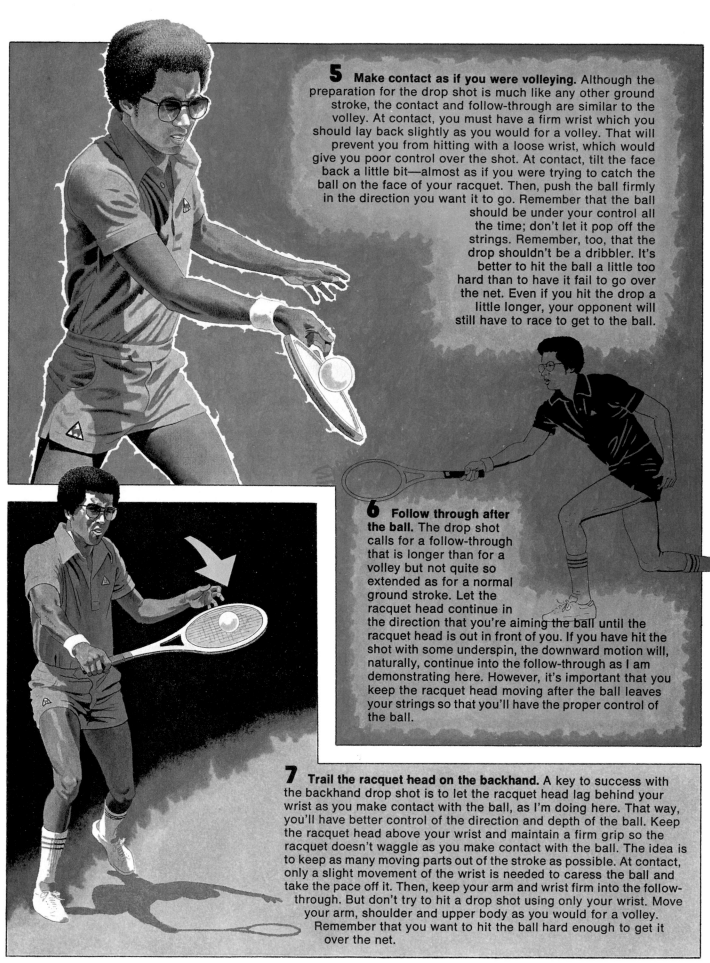

5 **Make contact as if you were volleying.** Although the preparation for the drop shot is much like any other ground stroke, the contact and follow-through are similar to the volley. At contact, you must have a firm wrist which you should lay back slightly as you would for a volley. That will prevent you from hitting with a loose wrist, which would give you poor control over the shot. At contact, tilt the face back a little bit—almost as if you were trying to catch the ball on the face of your racquet. Then, push the ball firmly in the direction you want it to go. Remember that the ball should be under your control all the time; don't let it pop off the strings. Remember, too, that the drop shouldn't be a dribbler. It's better to hit the ball a little too hard than to have it fail to go over the net. Even if you hit the drop a little longer, your opponent will still have to race to get to the ball.

6 **Follow through after the ball.** The drop shot calls for a follow-through that is longer than for a volley but not quite so extended as for a normal ground stroke. Let the racquet head continue in the direction that you're aiming the ball until the racquet head is out in front of you. If you have hit the shot with some underspin, the downward motion will, naturally, continue into the follow-through as I am demonstrating here. However, it's important that you keep the racquet head moving after the ball leaves your strings so that you'll have the proper control of the ball.

7 **Trail the racquet head on the backhand.** A key to success with the backhand drop shot is to let the racquet head lag behind your wrist as you make contact with the ball, as I'm doing here. That way, you'll have better control of the direction and depth of the ball. Keep the racquet head above your wrist and maintain a firm grip so the racquet doesn't waggle as you make contact with the ball. The idea is to keep as many moving parts out of the stroke as possible. At contact, only a slight movement of the wrist is needed to caress the ball and take the pace off it. Then, keep your arm and wrist firm into the follow-through. But don't try to hit a drop shot using only your wrist. Move your arm, shoulder and upper body as you would for a volley. Remember that you want to hit the ball hard enough to get it over the net.

8 **Recover quickly.** Your drop shots will almost always be hit from the no-man's-land area between the baseline and the service line. After you've hit the shot, you'll have a choice of going up to the net or retreating. Moving to the net is risky because your opponent will then have a good chance of lobbing over you if he can get to the ball. Your best bet is to backpedal a little way so you are close to the baseline but not behind it. By staying in front of the baseline, you'll be in a good position to be aggressive if your opponent makes a weak reply to your drop shot. Take advantage of the set-up position you've created.

9 **Use your ground strokes to complement your drop shot.** Chris Evert Lloyd has the finest drop shot in women's tennis today because she sets the trap for it so well and hits the shot as precisely as her other ground strokes. If you watch Chris play, you'll see that her ground strokes are always deep to keep her opponent pinned behind the baseline. Then, when her opponent hits a shorter ball, Chris is able to move in and hit a perfectly executed crosscourt drop shot that will send her opponent scrambling up to the net.

Often, Chris will force an error this way. Or, having brought her victim up to the net like a spider enticing a fly into its web, she will hit a winning passing shot. You should try to do the same—use your ground strokes to keep your opponent back and drop shot only when the right opportunity presents itself. Chris uses the drop as a surprise tactic. You can keep that element of surprise if you use the drop occasionally and well.

16 STEPS TO FASTER FOOTWORK

1 **The three key elements.** Because tennis is basically an instinctive game, a discussion of court movement can get enmeshed in such complex subjects as muscle memory and subconscious reactions. I prefer to keep things simple. So as I see it, good court movement really involves a combination of three elements: your eyes, your backswing and your feet. Put all those three together and your game will really start to move.

For instance, if your feet move swiftly in getting to the ball but you don't take your racquet back as you run or you don't watch the ball, the chances are you'll hit a poor shot. So good court movement is often a matter of coordination. Better movement involves improvement in watching the ball and stroking as well as agile footwork.

2 **Connect your eyes and your feet.** It may sound strange, but the key to speeding up your footwork is to make a better connection between your eyes and your feet. Take the situation where you are waiting for your opponent to serve. You should watch your opponent's ball toss carefully. As he lifts the ball, your reactions should follow instinctively.

If your eyes tell you that the ball is going to come to your right side, you've got to get the message through to your feet to push off from the left foot. Whether you have to take one step or several steps to get to the ball, the message should be the same: start moving (as I'm doing in the drawing at the left).

3 **Move the foot farthest from the ball.** Even when the ball is coming right to you, you still have to adjust yourself to get into position to hit the ball. Move the foot that's farthest away from the ball first. If I'm going for a backhand (see below), I move my right foot first. If I were to move my left foot first, my body would stop and I'd have to get it moving again. So I'd lose precious time. If the ball is coming to me, all I have to do is step out to meet the oncoming ball with my right foot, while turning on the ball of my left foot. That way, I can move my weight forward into the ball as I hit it.

4 **Skip for the close balls.** If you are preparing to hit a ball that's going to be only a few feet away, the fastest way to set yourself up for it is to skip sideways until you are ready to make that final step toward the oncoming ball. Begin by moving the foot that's farthest away from the ball and skip with short, quick steps like a boxer. Two or three steps is all that's needed to get to most balls, assuming that you were in the correct position for your opponent's shot. This kind of movement is difficult, I'll admit, so I suggest you practice in front of a full-length mirror. Use a racquet and do remember to take it back as you move.

5 **Run with your racquet back for wide balls.** When your opponent hits a ball that pulls you wide or when you are simply out of position, you'll have to turn and run for the ball. If you are a right-hander going for a forehand, as I'm demonstrating below, pivot on your right foot, cross over with your left and run with short, quick steps. Turning your body will start your racquet moving back. But keep drawing it back so that when you arrive at the point where you make your final step into the ball, you'll also be ready to begin your forward swing. As you move, keep your weight forward, leaning a little like a sprinter (below, right). You should still have your center of gravity forward when you make your stroke (below, left). By keeping your weight forward, you'll stay on your toes and, thus, move faster.

7 **Learn by watching other players.** I am a big fan of Ken Rosewall (left). He and Pancho Gonzalez had the best footwork I've ever seen. You can learn a lot from watching Rosewall move. Of course, he's relatively small and light, which helps. But Rosewall never wastes effort. He moves with such maximum efficiency that he always seems to have plenty of time to hit the ball. At tournaments some years ago, I'd sit in the stands and watch Rosewall's feet, particularly on the return of serve. He never bounced; he just watched the ball and took off after it with the precision of a surgeon and the speed of a sprinter. You, too, can learn from watching contemporary champions such as Bjorn Borg and Jimmy Connors, who both have exceptional footwork.

6 **Coordinate your backswing with your feet.** When players begin to think seriously about their footwork, there's a tendency to neglect the rest of the body. But the best footwork in the world won't help you hit the ball if your racquet is in the wrong place at the wrong time.

Run with your racquet moving back so you're ready to start your swing at the ball as you take your final step toward it. There should be no pause in your stroke between backswing and forward swing. Just as your feet should not stop moving, keep your racquet moving smoothly with no interruptions to affect your timing.

8 **Take small steps to position yourself for a smash.** Many players don't realize that footwork is a vital part of hitting an overhead smash. Most of the mistakes made with the smash are due to being in the wrong place—too close or too far from the dropping ball. For a smash, you must turn sideways to the flight of the ball and skip back into position using small steps. Then, as the ball comes closer, use even smaller steps to make final adjustments in your position.

That's especially important when you're playing outside where a small gust of wind can affect the flight of the ball at the last moment. I prefer to point at the ball using my hand like a gunsight so that I always keep the ball in front of me where I can both see it and hit it effectively.

9 **Step out to meet your volleys.** When you're playing at the net, you'll rarely have to move more than a step or so in either direction to cover your volleys. However, how you make that step is crucial. You should always step toward the ball with the foot that's closest to the net once you've turned sideways to prepare for the shot. For example, if I have to stretch out for a backhand volley, as in the drawing on the left, I step across with my right foot, turning my body at the same time. If I were to step with my left foot, I wouldn't be able to reach as far and I'd be cramping my stroke with my upper body.

Similarly, for a volley on the forehand side, I step out with my left foot. The principle's the same as for ground strokes: push off on the foot farthest away from the ball. If you do that, you'll make few footwork errors at the net.

10 **Remember to practice your footwork.** In your practice sessions, be sure to use proper footwork all the time, even for balls that you are casually returning for your partner to serve. Your footwork, as I said earlier, should become instinctive. It never will be if you're lax about it. But if you work at it, then when you need to move fast, your feet will respond without your having to think.

Jimmy Connors, for example, is almost as fast on his feet as Muhammed Ali, yet I'm sure he rarely thinks about his footwork. When he's in a tight spot, as with this low volley, he puts my three elements of eyes, feet and racquet together at the right place and time with absolutely no hesitation. That's what you, too, should aim for in getting your footwork grooved.

PART IV

THE SINGLES GAME

1 Use your head to win. When you watch the men pros play singles, the game often seems simple—just a matter of serving, rushing the net, hitting a couple of volleys and closing out the point. But for both the pro and the club player, the key to winning isn't just a slam-bang, power-hitting game. You'll win more singles matches against tough opponents if you understand some of the basic ideas of singles strategy. So I'm going to suggest some points that you can use in developing your own game plans. Remember, though, that these are not rules. If a particular idea doesn't work out for you, then change it. By using your head and playing smarter singles, you'll significantly increase your chances of winning.

2 Work to make your strokes consistent. It's obvious, but it needs to be said: a better command of singles strategy won't win you that many more matches unless you have consistent strokes. So work on developing a reliable serve, practice smooth and controlled ground strokes, and sharpen up your volleys. There's only one way to do that and it's through practice. Get yourself a partner and work together on the weaker strokes in your repertoires. Or, if you really hate to practice, make a conscious effort to use those weaker strokes whenever you play in a social match. Content yourself with just getting the ball back until the stroke improves. You should remember, too, that the guy who always gets the ball back will win the match.

3 **Get your first serve in.** That dictum ought to be stamped on every can of balls that you open. Your first serve should be your best serve—the one that will give your opponent the most trouble and may even win the point outright for you. Of course, if you miss your first serve, you'll be forced to use your weaker second serve and run the risk of double-faulting. So hit your first serve deep, preferably with a little spin to make sure that it doesn't go long, and you'll cut down the chances of your opponent hitting an aggressive service return.

4 **Follow your first serve to the net.** Singles is a game that can often be won or lost at the net, so you should generally try to follow your first serve to the net. (There are two exceptions: first, when you're facing a player with a terrific return of serve and, second, when you're playing on the slowest of clay courts which give an opponent time to tee off on your serve.)
Hit your first serve deep and start your move to the net immediately so that you get close to the "T" of the service boxes before you have to hit your first volley. Then, move in closer to the net to be in good shape to polish off the point with a second well-placed volley.

5 **Stay back on your second serve.** If you have to hit a second serve, it's best to stay back close to the baseline to wait for the return. Aim to get your second serve deep to your opponent's weakness. He or she may try to take advantage of your second serve by moving in a few steps and picking the ball off early. So you should recover quickly and be in a good ready position, prepared to move rapidly to get to the ball. If your opponent hits deep ground strokes, assume your ready position a couple of feet behind the baseline.

6 **Play it safe on returns.** When you're receiving serve, don't try anything fancy. Satisfy yourself with just getting the ball back over the net. And don't go for one of those net skimmers that look terrific when you hit them right, but more often than not wind up in the net. Besides, even if a net-skimmer is good, it will land so short in the other court that it will present your opponent with a perfect opportunity to move up to hit an approach shot and then take the net. So aim the ball at least three or four feet over the net to make it go deep in the other court and keep your opponent back on the baseline. Send most of your service returns crosscourt, too, where you've got more margin for error.

7 **Return crosscourt balls crosscourt.** You'll make fewer errors if you hit balls that come to you crosscourt back the same way. There are three reasons for that: first, you'll have more court in which to aim the ball; second, the ball will pass over the lowest point of the net; and third, you'll be returning the ball along roughly the same path that it came to you—which is easier than trying to alter the ball's direction to go down the line. Returning the ball down the line will open up the court, permitting your opponent to hit an angled crosscourt shot unless you can hit a ball that just clips the baseline.

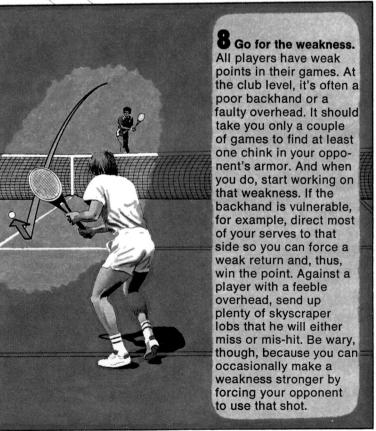

8 **Go for the weakness.** All players have weak points in their games. At the club level, it's often a poor backhand or a faulty overhead. It should take you only a couple of games to find at least one chink in your opponent's armor. And when you do, start working on that weakness. If the backhand is vulnerable, for example, direct most of your serves to that side so you can force a weak return and, thus, win the point. Against a player with a feeble overhead, send up plenty of skyscraper lobs that he will either miss or mis-hit. Be wary, though, because you can occasionally make a weakness stronger by forcing your opponent to use that shot.

9 Never let your opponent get in a groove. Some players like to camp out permanently on the baseline and send back a stream of deep crosscourt shots. When you are facing such an opponent, never let him get in a groove —he's just waiting for you to make the error that will give him the point. Remember that most tennis matches are decided by who makes the least errors, not the most winners. So mix up your shots to the steady baseliner. Hit some long balls and some short ones. Hit some shots crosscourt and others down the line. Above all, keep your opponent guessing so that you never let him develop his own rhythm which will force you to play his game. Make him play your game.

10 Bring in the steady baseliner. If your opponent prefers to play from the baseline and likes to engage in endless rallies, give him the shot that he'll hate. Hit a short ball that will force him to come to the net. Take a little pace off your own ground stroke and aim the ball lower over the net so that it bounces close to the service line. You're not trying to hit a drop shot (that's too risky from the baseline), just a short ball that will bring him in. The chances are that he'll be uncomfortable in the forecourt and will mis-hit the ball or give you an easy set-up.

11 Blunt the power of a hard hitter. When you are up against a player who blasts away at the ball with lusty ground strokes, one of the worst things you can do is to try to outpower him. If you hit the ball back hard, a power player will simply use the pace on the ball to return it yet harder so that it may shoot right by you. Instead, you should take the pace off the ball by returning it with a smooth, firm but relatively gentle stroke. That way, your opponent will have to generate his own pace every time and he'll tire before you do. I found this technique very effective against Jimmy Connors when I beat him in the 1975 Wimbledon final. It can work for you, too.

12 **Return spin with spin.** Many club players seem to have great difficulty in coping with balls that are spinning sharply. I think that's because they make the mistake of trying to take the spin off the ball. Why not use that spin and return spin with more spin? If a ball comes to you that is heavy with topspin, hit under the ball slightly so that you increase the spin and return the ball with underspin. Or if the ball is sliced to you with underspin, hit over the ball a little so that you return it with lots of topspin. You'll be adding more spin to the ball instead of trying to reverse the spin.

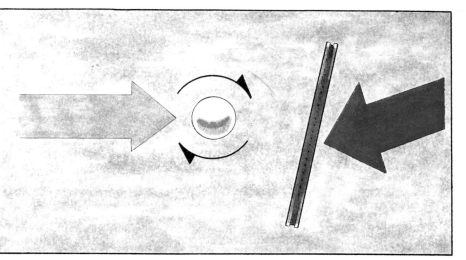

13 **Use your lob against a net-rusher.** Too many singles players forget that the lob is just as useful in singles as in doubles. You should not only lob against the player with a weak overhead; you should also use the lob to force a net-rusher away from the net. Both the defensive and offensive lobs have their places in singles play. If you are out of position, launch a high, deep defensive lob that will take your opponent back to the baseline and give you enough time to recover. If your opponent is crowding the net, try a quick offensive lob just out of his reach as an alternative to a passing shot. A good offensive lob may win the point outright for you.

14 **Follow a short ball to the net.** When your opponent hits a shot that lands closer to the service line than the baseline, you should dart forward to the ball, hit a deep approach shot and continue on up to the net ready to put away your opponent's return with a volley. Most of your approach shots should go down the line and you should then shift your position to cover a possible down-the-line passing shot by your opponent. By doing that, you'll pressure your opponent into attempting the more difficult crosscourt passing shot. And he probably won't be able to pass you crosscourt because you'll have time to move over and cut off the shot. So when your opportunity comes to charge forward, keep moving up to that net position.

15 **Hit your first volleys deep.** Whether you are following your first serve or an approach shot to the net, you should aim your first volleys as deep as possible. A deep volley will force your opponent to stay back at the baseline, which will give you a chance to score with a winning second volley off his return. Concentrate on hitting down on your first volley and meeting the ball firmly and easily. Make sure, too, that you pause for that first volley; if you are still running forward at contact, you may hit the ball off balance and, thus, mess up the shot. After contact, you can continue moving toward the net to prepare for the next volley.

16 **Keep moving to follow your volleys.** Singles net play is tougher than doubles if only because you have more area to cover—on your own. That means your anticipation must be sharper and you have to be quick on your feet to foil your opponent's attempts at hitting a passing shot out of your reach. So whenever you hit a volley, anticipate the return by gliding a little in the direction in which you hit your volley. That will put you closer to the center of your opponent's possible angles of return where you'll have the best chance to intercept his shot. Don't wait for your opponent to hit the ball; start moving as soon as you've hit your volley. And keep moving at the net.

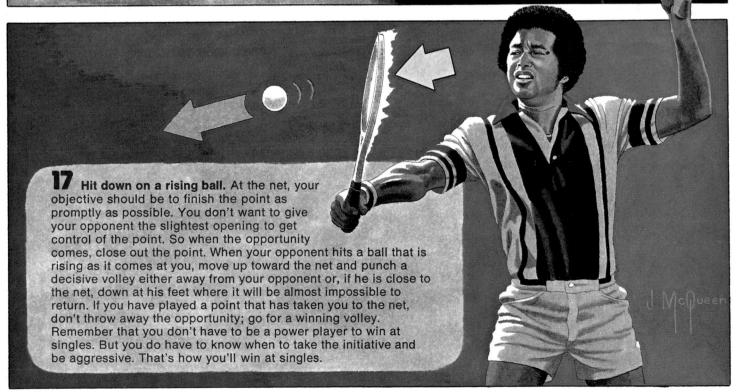

17 **Hit down on a rising ball.** At the net, your objective should be to finish the point as promptly as possible. You don't want to give your opponent the slightest opening to get control of the point. So when the opportunity comes, close out the point. When your opponent hits a ball that is rising as it comes at you, move up toward the net and punch a decisive volley either away from your opponent or, if he is close to the net, down at his feet where it will be almost impossible to return. If you have played a point that has taken you to the net, don't throw away the opportunity; go for a winning volley. Remember that you don't have to be a power player to win at singles. But you do have to know when to take the initiative and be aggressive. That's how you'll win at singles.

18 PLAYING PERCENTAGE TENNIS

1 **What is percentage tennis?**
Playing the percentages is one of the fundamentals of successful tennis. It means that, in any situation, you would use the shot that has the greatest chance of success. For example, how often does the guy with the big booming first serve get it in? Maybe one time in 10 if he's lucky. That's a 10 percent chance of success. When the boomer eases off on his serve, the percentage of good serves might go up to 60 percent or more. So, when you need the point, say at 30-40, you use the serve that has the greatest chance of going in. At 40-love, you can risk the cannonball. That's playing the percentages. Another way of looking at percentage tennis is to play in a way that will make the most of your strengths and minimize your weaknesses. If you have a great lob, use it when the going gets tough. If your overhead is for the birds, let the ball bounce and hit a forehand. The percentages are different for every player, but I can give you a few ideas that will help you work out the percentages for your own game.

2 **Get your first serve in.** Nothing improves your chance of winning so much as simply getting your first serve in play. When you go for the ace and miss, the pressure mounts on your second serve. You'll not only be apprehensive about getting it in, but your opponent will probably be gleefully anticipating a blooper that he can pounce on easily. So get your first serve in by taking some speed off it and using a little more spin. It won't be a cannonball, but it sure will be tougher to handle than your usual patsy of a second serve. Get that first serve in and you'll be in a much more commanding position for the rest of the point, whether you are going to the net or staying back. And that goes double for doubles. With a good first serve, you'll be able to go to the net every time—unless you're up against a player with a blistering return of serve like Jimmy Connors.

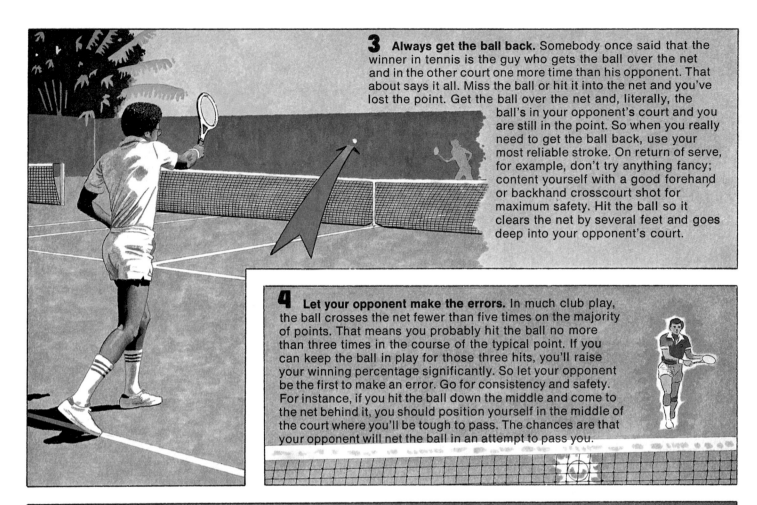

3 **Always get the ball back.** Somebody once said that the winner in tennis is the guy who gets the ball over the net and in the other court one more time than his opponent. That about says it all. Miss the ball or hit it into the net and you've lost the point. Get the ball over the net and, literally, the ball's in your opponent's court and you are still in the point. So when you really need to get the ball back, use your most reliable stroke. On return of serve, for example, don't try anything fancy; content yourself with a good forehand or backhand crosscourt shot for maximum safety. Hit the ball so it clears the net by several feet and goes deep into your opponent's court.

4 **Let your opponent make the errors.** In much club play, the ball crosses the net fewer than five times on the majority of points. That means you probably hit the ball no more than three times in the course of the typical point. If you can keep the ball in play for those three hits, you'll raise your winning percentage significantly. So let your opponent be the first to make an error. Go for consistency and safety. For instance, if you hit the ball down the middle and come to the net behind it, you should position yourself in the middle of the court where you'll be tough to pass. The chances are that your opponent will net the ball in an attempt to pass you.

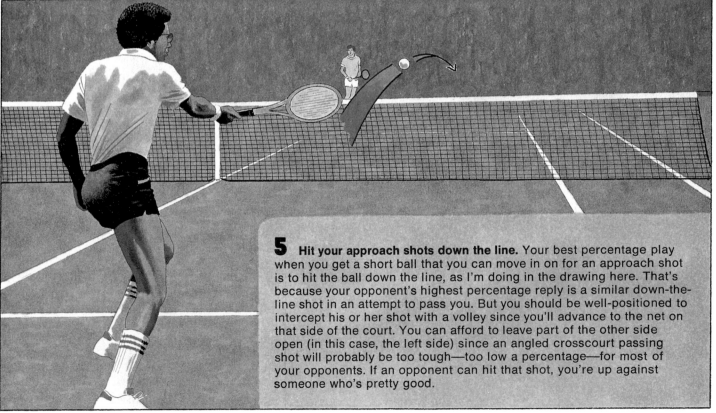

5 **Hit your approach shots down the line.** Your best percentage play when you get a short ball that you can move in on for an approach shot is to hit the ball down the line, as I'm doing in the drawing here. That's because your opponent's highest percentage reply is a similar down-the-line shot in an attempt to pass you. But you should be well-positioned to intercept his or her shot with a volley since you'll advance to the net on that side of the court. You can afford to leave part of the other side open (in this case, the left side) since an angled crosscourt passing shot will probably be too tough—too low a percentage—for most of your opponents. If an opponent can hit that shot, you're up against someone who's pretty good.

6 **Angle your drop shots.** The drop shot, like an approach shot, should be hit off a ball that lands well inside the baseline. But instead of going down the line, the best percentage play with a drop shot is to angle it crosscourt. There are a couple of reasons for that. First, you'll be hitting the ball over the center part of the net where it's lowest. And second, you'll be hitting away from your opponent most of the time and making him run the greatest distance to reach the ball. Also, because the ball is traveling more laterally than it would be if you hit it down the middle or down the line, it will stay closer to the net. And the shorter the distance your ball travels past the net, the more difficulty your opponent will have in returning the ball. You'll be forcing him to hit up, presenting you with an opportunity to hit down for a winner. Remember that the drop shot is rarely an outright winner; your best bet is to use it to set up a winning situation.

7 **Favor your best service return.** Most club players have a better forehand than backhand return of serve. If that's the case with you, leave the forehand side open slightly when you prepare to return serve. If you're a right-hander facing a right-handed server in the deuce court, that means moving a foot or two to the left (see below, left) instead of standing close to the singles sideline. In the ad court, move closer to the alley than your normal receiving position (below, right). By leaving the forehand side open, you invite the server to hit to that side instead of the backhand which is conventional wisdom for most club players. If he does serve to your backhand, you will be right there and ready to return. If he goes to the forehand side, you can move quickly and hit the return with your best shot.

8 **Hit your overheads crosscourt.** When you hit an overhead smash, you should be trying to win the point either directly or by forcing an error. At the same time, you must be sure you do not make an error yourself. So I suggest that you should hit your overheads crosscourt where you'll have the most room and, hence, the greatest margin for error. You'll probably win the point outright. But even if your opponent manages to get his racquet on the ball, the return will be weak and you'll be able to put it away easily. To cover the possibility of a down-the-line return, move over to the side to which you hit your overhead. Even when you are smashing from deep in your court, your overheads should still go crosscourt. However, it's more likely that your opponent will be able to return a smash hit from one baseline to the other, so be ready to move for that down-the-line return in case your opponent gets to the ball.

J. McQueen

9 **When you're deep behind the baseline, use your lob.** There are times when your opponent puts you on the defensive by hitting a deep ball that pushes you way behind your baseline. From that position, you can't hope to hit an offensive drive or a passing shot, especially if your opponent is at the net. Your best percentage shot is to hit a high, deep defensive lob crosscourt. The deep lob will give you time to recover for your next shot and will force your opponent back behind his own baseline. You're less likely to make an error with a lob than another shot. That's percentage tennis: playing an error-free game.

19 ADJUSTING TO DIFFERENT COURT SURFACES

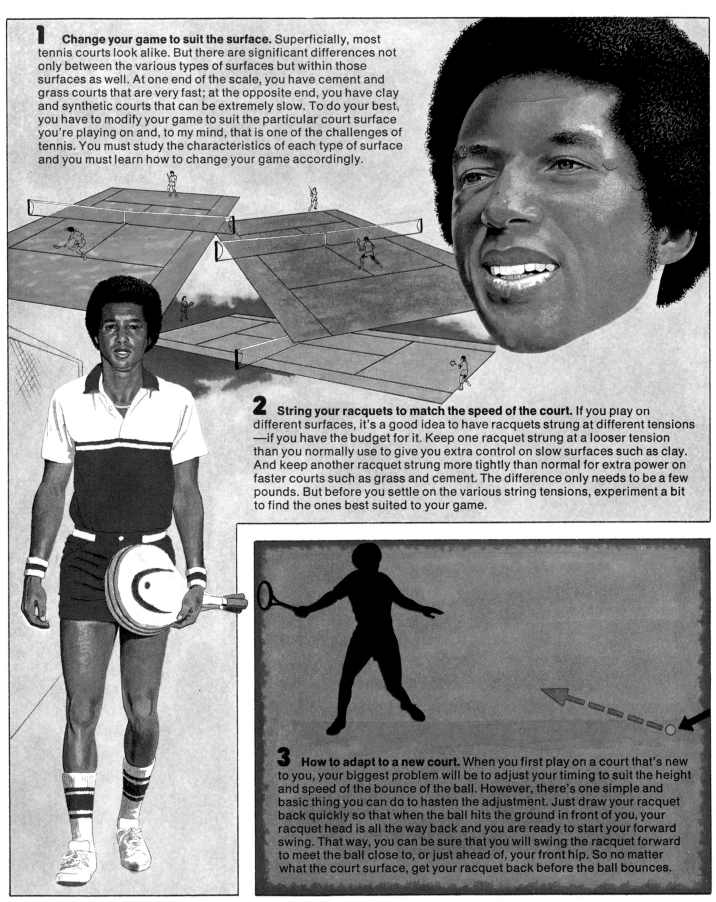

1 **Change your game to suit the surface.** Superficially, most tennis courts look alike. But there are significant differences not only between the various types of surfaces but within those surfaces as well. At one end of the scale, you have cement and grass courts that are very fast; at the opposite end, you have clay and synthetic courts that can be extremely slow. To do your best, you have to modify your game to suit the particular court surface you're playing on and, to my mind, that is one of the challenges of tennis. You must study the characteristics of each type of surface and you must learn how to change your game accordingly.

2 **String your racquets to match the speed of the court.** If you play on different surfaces, it's a good idea to have racquets strung at different tensions —if you have the budget for it. Keep one racquet strung at a looser tension than you normally use to give you extra control on slow surfaces such as clay. And keep another racquet strung more tightly than normal for extra power on faster courts such as grass and cement. The difference only needs to be a few pounds. But before you settle on the various string tensions, experiment a bit to find the ones best suited to your game.

3 **How to adapt to a new court.** When you first play on a court that's new to you, your biggest problem will be to adjust your timing to suit the height and speed of the bounce of the ball. However, there's one simple and basic thing you can do to hasten the adjustment. Just draw your racquet back quickly so that when the ball hits the ground in front of you, your racquet head is all the way back and you are ready to start your forward swing. That way, you can be sure that you will swing the racquet forward to meet the ball close to, or just ahead of, your front hip. So no matter what the court surface, get your racquet back before the ball bounces.

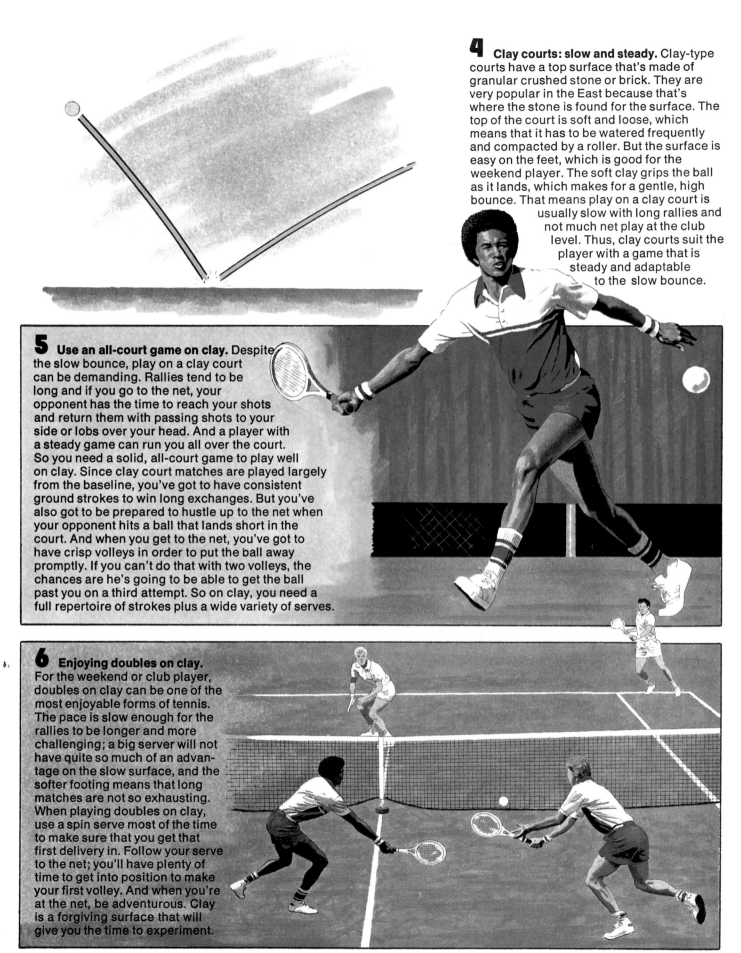

4 **Clay courts: slow and steady.** Clay-type courts have a top surface that's made of granular crushed stone or brick. They are very popular in the East because that's where the stone is found for the surface. The top of the court is soft and loose, which means that it has to be watered frequently and compacted by a roller. But the surface is easy on the feet, which is good for the weekend player. The soft clay grips the ball as it lands, which makes for a gentle, high bounce. That means play on a clay court is usually slow with long rallies and not much net play at the club level. Thus, clay courts suit the player with a game that is steady and adaptable to the slow bounce.

5 **Use an all-court game on clay.** Despite the slow bounce, play on a clay court can be demanding. Rallies tend to be long and if you go to the net, your opponent has the time to reach your shots and return them with passing shots to your side or lobs over your head. And a player with a steady game can run you all over the court. So you need a solid, all-court game to play well on clay. Since clay court matches are played largely from the baseline, you've got to have consistent ground strokes to win long exchanges. But you've also got to be prepared to hustle up to the net when your opponent hits a ball that lands short in the court. And when you get to the net, you've got to have crisp volleys in order to put the ball away promptly. If you can't do that with two volleys, the chances are he's going to be able to get the ball past you on a third attempt. So on clay, you need a full repertoire of strokes plus a wide variety of serves.

6 **Enjoying doubles on clay.** For the weekend or club player, doubles on clay can be one of the most enjoyable forms of tennis. The pace is slow enough for the rallies to be longer and more challenging; a big server will not have quite so much of an advantage on the slow surface, and the softer footing means that long matches are not so exhausting. When playing doubles on clay, use a spin serve most of the time to make sure that you get that first delivery in. Follow your serve to the net; you'll have plenty of time to get into position to make your first volley. And when you're at the net, be adventurous. Clay is a forgiving surface that will give you the time to experiment.

7 **Cement courts: fast and furious.** Almost at the opposite end of the scale from clay courts are the hard cement courts that are most common in the West. Because the cement is so hard, the ball bounces relatively high (although not as high as on clay)— and loses little speed in the bounce. So the pace of play on cement is fast. Fortunately, some cement courts have a top layer that is designed to slow the ball down and, thus, reduce the swiftness of the exchanges. So you may find quite a variation in speed between cement courts. Some can be so slick that the ball almost skids across the surface and stays fairly low. On others, the rough surface grabs the ball so that it bounces higher and is slowed down. Generally, though, you have to get your racquet head back earlier on cement than on clay because the ball will be upon you sooner. Play warily at first in order to get a feel for the speed of the court.

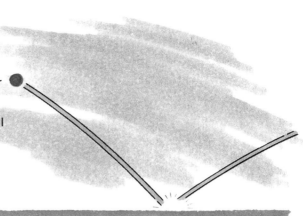

8 **Serve and volley on cement.** Cement courts place a premium on the serve-and-volley game. You'll do well on cement if you have a good, deep first serve (preferably with some spin) and the agility to get to the service line before you have to hit your first volley. Above all, get your first serve in on cement. Since the ball bounces relatively high, a weak second serve will be an easy set-up for a good receiver. A powerful serve is an advantage on cement, of course, but accuracy and spin are more important. If you can place the serve deep with spin, the chances are the receiver will hit a relatively weak return so that your first volley will be easier. In fact, you may be able to hit a winning first volley.

9 **Return serve carefully on a faster court.** On faster surfaces, such as cement and grass, aim for a safe, consistent return of serve. Just be satisfied with getting the ball back (crosscourt is best since it's over the lowest part of the net) either deep to a server who stays back or at the feet of a server who is rushing the net. On cement, a player with a spin serve may make the ball bounce quite high, meaning you have to meet it almost at shoulder level. Those are the hardest returns to make consistently. On grass, the reverse happens: the ball stays low and you have to dig it out with your racquet to get it back over the net. So just get your returns back every time.

10 **Indoor courts: custom-made and consistent.** Without any doubt, the boom in indoor courts is one of the greatest things to have happened to U.S. tennis in the last decade. While there are many types of indoor courts, most of them are either slow or medium-speed surfaces suited to the games of the average player. And most of them require little maintenance, meaning the courts perform the same way week in and week out. The conditions, moreover, are always the same. There is no sun or wind to bother about; the courts are heated in the winter and often air-conditioned in the summer.

11 **Watch those lobs indoors.** Having said that indoor courts are near-perfect for tennis, I should add one warning: watch the roof. You need to take a little extra care with your lobs indoors to be sure that you don't hit the roof or the suspended lights. That's not to say that you should avoid using your lob. On the contrary, if you play doubles you'll have to use the lob because it's an essential part of the game. But when you do lob, go for maximum control by keeping the ball on your racquet strings for as long as possible and following through completely. You'll find the lower offensive lob particularly useful indoors.

12 **Grass courts: rapid and rare.** I've left grass courts for last because they're almost museum pieces nowadays. Still, grass is the surface on which tennis got started and on which the world's premier tournament, Wimbledon, is played. Unfortunately, since the surface is expensive to put down and maintain, grass courts are disappearing. But if you can find one—play on it. Grass is the supreme experience of tennis, especially on a cloudless summer day. When you play on grass, you can expect the pace to be fast. The ball will skid across the surface and stay low. And you'll have the added difficulty of countering bad bounces (no grass court is perfect, even at Wimbledon). If you can, try your serve-and-volley game on grass. The points will be over quickly, but you'll be exhilarated —I guarantee it.

J. McQueen

1 **The all-important difference.** In any keenly-fought match, there are certain points that determine whether the momentum of play flows with you—or against you. If you can win these big points, you'll gain something more than a mere numerical advantage—you'll be psychologically ahead, too. Your opponent will realize that, when push comes to shove, you can pull out the little extra that will win you the critical points.

All the great tennis champions have this ability. Bjorn Borg, for one, possesses it to an extraordinary degree; he seems to know instinctively which are the significant points and can raise his game to win them. Is it possible for you to develop the same knack? To a certain extent, it definitely is. The first step is to learn to recognize what the big points are in a match—and I'll tell you how to do that. The second step, of course, is to appreciate what's necessary to win those points—and I'll have some suggestions on that, too.

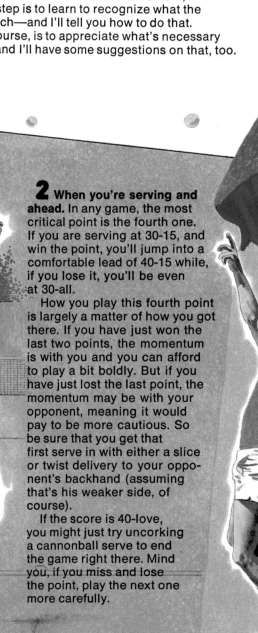

2 **When you're serving and ahead.** In any game, the most critical point is the fourth one. If you are serving at 30-15, and win the point, you'll jump into a comfortable lead of 40-15 while, if you lose it, you'll be even at 30-all.

How you play this fourth point is largely a matter of how you got there. If you have just won the last two points, the momentum is with you and you can afford to play a bit boldly. But if you have just lost the last point, the momentum may be with your opponent, meaning it would pay to be more cautious. So be sure that you get that first serve in with either a slice or twist delivery to your opponent's backhand (assuming that's his weaker side, of course).

If the score is 40-love, you might just try uncorking a cannonball serve to end the game right there. Mind you, if you miss and lose the point, play the next one more carefully.

3 **When you're serving and behind.** There are two critical points when you serve and are behind: 15-30 and ad-out. At 15-30, if you lose the next point, you'll be at 15-40, the momentum will be against you and the chances are that you'll lose the game. At ad out, if you lose the point you'll lose the game. So in both cases, the pressure is on you to win the point. How can you increase your chances of doing it? By thinking ahead about how you're going to play the point and trying to use your best shots. Since I'm a serve-and-volley player, for instance, I might decide to serve to the backhand, come in and attempt to hit an outright winner with a crosscourt volley.

4 **When you're receiving serve.** The biggest point when you're receiving serve is the first point of the game. A server normally expects to win his service game, while you're hoping for a break of serve. So if you can win the opening point of the game, you'll have gained a very important psychological advantage. Here's a good time to be a little more aggressive; after all, the worst that can happen is that you'll lose the point—which the odds are you'll do, anyway. So try something different. If you've been returning serve hard and deep, chip the ball gently and come in after it. Your opponent may be caught off guard and the point could soon be yours. Your other critical point when you receive occurs at 30-all. Here again, I'd take a few chances. The pressure's on the server to avoid falling behind by 30-40, so he'll probably use his most dependable serve. Move in a little and attack it to prevent him from advancing and hitting a good volley. You might even follow your return to net.

5 **When you have a chance to break serve.** If you are receiving and the score stands at 30-40, your ad or even deuce, you are really in a strong position. Capitalize on it! First, remember that the server must have made at least a couple of mistakes; he has to have done that to let you get to this point. Recall what those mistakes were and try to give him enough rope to hang himself with them again. Concentrate on playing as steadily as you can and letting the server make the error that will give you the point and, perhaps, the game, too.

When John Newcombe was about to break an opponent, I could almost predict that he would run around his backhand and blast a service return with that powerful forehand of his. Some players were so afraid of that big forehand that they would even double fault trying too hard to hit a serve away from it. So if the crosscourt forehand is your best return, too, use it to make sure you get the ball back safely.

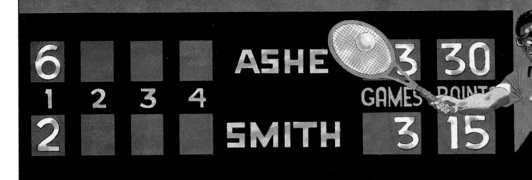

6 **Go for it in seventh games.** The big game in a set is the seventh—whether the score is 5-1, 4-2 or 3-all. The seventh game is one you should go all out to win—as the server or receiver. At 3-all, I prefer to serve and gain the mental edge of being 4-3 ahead, knowing that if I get a break I'll then be able to serve for the set. But if I'm receiving at 3-all, that's the time I go for a service break so that all I'll have to do from there is hold serve twice for the set.

So in the seventh game, and particularly when the score is even, pull out all the stops. Add a little extra spin or more speed to your serve to make sure you win the game decisively. If you are receiving, play with your opponent's head a little. By being bold, you'll make him think he stands a good chance of losing his serve and, probably, the set. Great players like Ken Rosewall and Rod Laver would simply crank up their games another notch in this game by piling on the pressure with aggressive serves and returns. You should do the same.

7 **Stay cool on match point.** Ironically, perhaps the toughest moments can come when you hold a set or match point—especially in a close contest. You're so near, yet so far. And your opponent, with his back to the wall, is invariably bearing down hard. To avoid choking, take your time and mentally plan out the point. Get your first serve in good and deep so you don't have to use your weaker second serve and, perhaps, run the risk of double-faulting. Even Bjorn Borg has to get his first serve in at match point. Both Borg and Chris Evert Lloyd (left) excel on set and match points because they go for the shots they're confident they can make. In Chrissie's case, that's often a two-fisted backhand. She knows she can stay back against an aggressive player like Martina Navratilova and wait for her to make an error. That's the other key to winning match point, of course: no errors. You don't need to do anything special to take that last point. Just play the same way you have been doing all along.

8 Play confidently in tiebreakers. Who can ever forget the incomparable tiebreaker that John McEnroe (left) won over Bjorn Borg at Wimbledon in 1980? If anyone does, John has the one quality that's needed above all others to prevail in a tiebreaker—confidence. When you've won six games to get to the tiebreaker, you should believe that you have what it takes to pull out this last game.

I prefer to receive serve on the first point in a 12-point tiebreaker because, even if I lose it, I then have the next two serves coming and a good chance to go ahead 2-1. However, the biggest point is the seventh —especially in a nine-point tiebreaker. If the score is 4-2 in your favor, the next point could decide the match. Even if the score is 3-all, I'd much rather be the one who is ahead 4-3. So if you are serving, the cardinal rule applies: get that first serve in. If you are receiving, try to break the serve to put yourself at 4-3 with two serves to come.

9 Learn from the pros. Bjorn Borg (right) is, without question, the greatest player of the big points today. He has such tremendous self-confidence in himself that, when he gets to a critical point, he knows he has the ability to hit any one shot he wants to hit.

Watch Borg on the important points. He will take his time in deciding how to serve and then play out the point with the precision of a surgeon. Borg, you'll notice, rarely takes an unnecessary risk on a critical point. He'll play just the way he's been doing throughout the match. The only way to beat a player like that is to do something that he's not expecting in order to jolt him out of his sense of assurance that he has you beaten.

Borg has another quality that helps him on the big points: his extraordinary concentration. And he can maintain it for unusually long periods, which means he is rarely disturbed by poor calls or noisy spectators. So do what you can to cultivate those two qualities of confidence and concentration. They'll go a long way toward helping you win your own critical points.

1 The joy of winning. A tournament is a challenging and a demanding occasion, for the club player as well as the professional. Of course, a typical pro enters 20 or more tournaments a year, while you might compete in two or three. So relatively speaking, your club tournament can mean as much to you as Wimbledon does to a pro. And I'm sure that you'd get the same kind of kick out of winning as I did when I captured my Wimbledon title.

Make no mistake about it, though. Winning a tournament is entirely different from winning your usual weekly doubles match. For one thing, you'll have to play several matches in a short space of time. For another, you'll likely be facing opponents whose games are new to you. So what I'd like to do in the next few pages is to give you some ideas that might help tip the odds of winning in your favor. There's nothing quite like the thrill you get from winning, so it's worth a little work and planning.

2 Set up a practice plan. For two or three weeks before your tournament, organize a practice program. Take a moment to write down the strengths and weaknesses of your game. If you're not sure about them, ask your regular partners or opponents; they'll soon be able to tell you! Start out by practicing your strongest strokes. That may sound a trifle odd, but the key here is to go into the tournament feeling utterly confident. Your strengths can compensate for your weaknesses because you will always have solid strokes you can fall back on when the going gets tough.

When your good strokes are really working for you, that's the time to devote more effort to your weaker points. The confidence you get from your strong strokes will help you work on your weaknesses, too.

Practice even when you play in your regular games. Set yourself a goal—such as no errors on your backhand for a game, a set or even a match. Better to lose to your friends than to lose in the first round of a tournament. If your strokes improve, a loss to friends is worth it.

3 **Get in shape.** I can't emphasize too much the necessity to be in peak physical condition as you go into a tournament. You are going to play several matches in a few days. While that is not a novelty for the pros, it is for most club players. So do a little more running in the month before your event. Increase those stretching exercises you should be doing every day and, if you are a tad overweight, get down to that diet you've been promising to follow the last few years.

Just as you might tune up your car for the big summer vacation, your body needs tuning for the extra stress of the tournament. Few club players train for the local tournament. If you can do it, you'll be one step ahead of the field when the first round starts.

4 **Know your tournament.** If the event is being played at your local club or town courts, you're in good shape. You'll already know the courts and how they play. However, the tournament may be held on unfamiliar courts. If so, check out the site before the big day comes. If you can, arrange to play on the actual courts so you can get a feel for the speed and bounce of the ball. At the very least, find out the name of the surface and ask how it compares to the courts you usually play on.

Find out, too, about the balls to be used. Are they heavier or lighter than your usual brand? How will they perform on the courts you'll be using? Again, try to play with the same balls on the same courts. While you are scouting the site, look around for such facilities as refreshment counters and locker rooms.

5 **Check out your gear.** At least a week before the tournament, check all the equipment you'll be taking to the event. You expect to be in top shape, and your equipment should be, too. You should have at least two, and preferably three, racquets. Have one of the racquets strung at a couple of pounds higher tension than usual in case damp conditions expand the gut during the tournament. Get your racquets restrung if there is any sign of fraying where the strings cross or at the string holes. Tell your stringer that you are playing in a tournament and may need a rush job if one of your strings should break. Replace the grips if they are slick and worn.

Take a look at your shoes. Do they need new laces? A second pair may come in handy. Check out your tennis bag, too. Do you have enough sweatbands? How about a small towel, Band-Aids, sunscreen and so on?

6 **Warm up before you play.** Plan to arrive well ahead of the scheduled time of your first match so you can get organized and have plenty of time to warm up. Do some gentle stretching exercises to loosen up the muscles followed by a little jogging and a few sprints to get the heart and lungs moving.

You may also want to hit some balls with a friend or another player if you can find a free court. However, don't work so hard before your match that you sweat too much and then cool down before play begins. Start your warm-up about 15 minutes before the match and that should be about right.

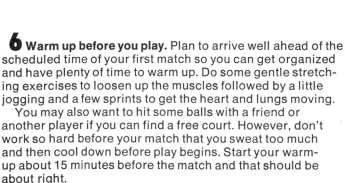

7 **Play steadily as the match starts.** For the first few games, don't go for winners. Simply play steadily to get into a groove. Get your first serves in, preferably with depth. If your opponent looks weak on the backhand, serve mostly to that side. When you return serve, just concentrate on getting the ball back over the net. Remember that your opponent is probably just as nervous as you are—and equally likely to make mistakes.

Tell yourself that you are not going to make errors, even if you have to bloop the ball back over the net until you get into your stride. In club play, matches are won on errors, not winners. So the fewer errors you make, the more points you'll win.

8 **Go back to basics in an emergency.** If your game begins to fall apart, go back to the basics. Take a little off your first serve to make sure it goes in. If you don't get your first serve in, the chances are your opponent will really tee off on your weak second serve. If your volleying is erratic, stay back and be content to play steadily from the baseline. If you are consistently missing overheads, let the ball bounce and take it with a ground stroke.

The objective here is to repair your damaged confidence and get back into the game. Of course, you may be up against a player who simply is much better than you. When that's the case, don't give up. Play your best and, if you have to, lose with honor. After any match, win or lose, you should feel that you played your best.

9 **Ignore spectators.** If you are not used to playing in front of an audience, I have one suggestion to make: remember that the crowd is not hitting any balls—you are. Just ignore the crowd and get on with the business of playing the match. Sure, there are pressures in playing in front of a crowd; but if you can't put up with the heat, get out of the kitchen.

I learned early in my career to control my emotions on the court both toward my opponent and the crowds. I think my composure on the court essentially won many matches for me. Not that you have to maintain a Bjorn Borg-like poker face. You can let your emotions surface. But retain control of yourself so you can concentrate on the match.

10 **Learn from your matches.** In any singles tournament, obviously only one player, the champion, is going to be undefeated. Everybody else will lose eventually. In fact, if you are new to the tournament game, you may lose all the time at first. But don't get discouraged —even great players had to lose before they started winning.

Look upon each tournament as an experience from which you can learn. I recommend that you keep a notebook in which you can jot down points to remember or to work on and which you can refer to as you progress. And you will progress if you always play your best. After a match, you should be able to say to yourself: "Well, I lost but I did what I was supposed to do."

If your game plan didn't work, then it just didn't work. But maybe you learned a few points that will help you the next time. If your attitude is right, you will begin to win matches and, who knows, it may be you accepting the trophy next time.

PART V
THE DOUBLES GAME

22 WINNING DOUBLES TACTICS

1 **A game for all seasons.** Doubles is really the fun version of tennis. Whereas singles is often an intense struggle between two equally determined opponents, doubles is much more of a social game—even when played competitively.

But because there are more players on the court, doubles can often be a more difficult game to play. First of all, two players have to act as a team, which is tough if they have big egos or differ greatly in ability.

More importantly, though, the strategies of play are not the same for doubles and singles. And that's why you have some fine doubles teams with good strategists, like Bob Hewitt and Frew McMillan, who are relatively undistinguished in singles. However, I've always enjoyed both versions of the sport. In fact, one of the great thrills of my career was winning the French Open men's doubles title in 1971 with that master of doubles play, Marty Riessen.

2 **Pick your partner carefully.** Your first crucial decision in doubles should be made off the court—selecting your partner. Look for a person who will be a team player, rather than a flashy individualist who will hog the court, take the credit when you win and give you the blame when you lose.

The greatest doubles pairs on the pro circuit—such teams as Stan Smith and Bob Lutz (right), Tom Okker and Wojtek Fibak, or Hewitt and McMillan—do not play flashy doubles. They concentrate instead on getting the ball back and letting their opponents make most of the errors.

Of course, the player you choose should also have good all-around tennis skills. A big weapon like a cannonball serve is not as important in doubles as in singles. But it's best if you both have a wide repertoire of strokes.

3 **Make your first serve good.**
The serving team should always hold its serve.
After all, you need only one break of serve to win a set. But if you lose your serve, you'll need at least another break. So there's no sense in giving points away with faults. You don't need a punishing first serve however. The best serve for doubles is a deep, well-controlled spin serve that will slice away from the receiver, presenting him with a hard ball to hit. And the slightly slower speed will give you that valuable extra time to get to the net.

If you fail to get your first serve in, the pressure on your second serve will be enormous. Chances are, you'll go for a blooper of a serve that the receiver will pounce on and hammer back at your shoelaces. That, you don't need. But if you invariably get your first serve in, the receiver will respect your serve and you'll keep the advantage that will help you win the point and your service game.

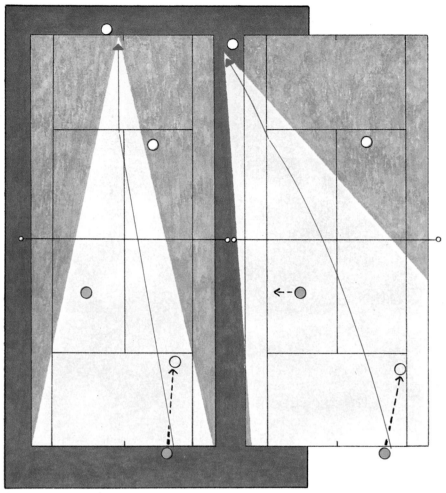

4 **Serve down the middle of the court.** In doubles, control of the middle of the court is the name of the game. If your opponents can hit crafty angled shots down the alleys, they're too good and deserve to win the points. But you can defeat even skilled opponents if you keep the ball in the middle by serving mostly down the center of the court, whether you are serving from the deuce (right side) or ad (left side) court.

For example, if you serve down the center into the deuce court (far left), the receiver's choice of angles is limited mostly to the middle (shaded area) which can easily be controlled by you and your partner. But if you serve wide into the deuce court (left) the receiver has a larger choice of angles and you'll have a tougher time controlling the point. With the wide serve, a good player can angle the ball over into the server's alley or he can pass the net man down the line. It's unlikely that either you or your partner will be speedy enough to cover those possibilities.

5 **Follow your serve to the net.** Provided you get that first serve in, you should always come to the net. If you can gain control there, you can usually expect to win the point.

On your way to the net, don't try for a winning shot on your first volley. If the receiver returns crosscourt (which he should do most of the time), hit a well-controlled volley deep down the middle out of reach of the other team's net man. You can then move in closer to the net to prepare for your next volley. Don't get too close, however, in case you have to retreat quickly for a lob over your head.

You should stay back only if you have a weak second serve or if you are playing someone with a crackerjack return of serve. In the latter case, I'd suggest that you both play back for the return and move in later.

6 **Use extra spin on your second serve.** No one bats 1.000 on their first serves, of course. So you need a reasonably potent second serve for doubles. Here's where you're looking for some insurance. The second serve has to go in or you give the point away.

So I suggest that you put some extra spin on the serve—first, to make sure that the serve curves down into the service box, and second, to give the receiver a tougher target to hit. You may also want to serve from a little closer to the singles sideline so you can aim directly at the receiver. A ball coming directly at a player is much harder to return than one an arm's length away.

7 **Be prepared to cover lobs on your side.** If you and your partner cover the middle of the court effectively at the net, you'll leave your opponents with a couple of options: to go down the alleys or to hit over your heads. Going for the alleys with two players close to the net is a low percentage shot. So an experienced doubles team will often resort to the lob.

When that happens, the cardinal rule is to handle all the lobs on your side of the court. Don't expect your partner to cover for you. If the lob is on your side, yell out, "Mine!" And then get into position as quickly as you can. If the lob is relatively short, hit your overhead before the ball bounces and move back up to the net position. If the lob is high and deep, run back, let the ball bounce and then hit a deep ground stroke or smash return.

If a lob forces you back behind the baseline, stay there until you get the short ball that will let you move up. Your partner should not retreat with you for a short lob, but should be ready to accompany you back to the baseline if the lob is deep and you have to stay back.

8 **Try poaching—you'll like it.** When you are facing a player with a fairly predictable return of serve, that's the time to attempt a poach. That's when the net man moves over quickly to cut off a service return with a sharp volley that's aimed out of the reach of the other team or down at the other net man's feet. Either way, the result should be a point won by the poacher.

Poaching is fun and not too difficult, if you go about it the right way. You must first agree with your partner when the poach will take place—say, on return of a serve to the deuce court. The poacher must then start to move just before the receiver hits the ball. If he waits to see where the return is going, he'll be too late. And as the net man poaches, the server must cross over behind him just in case the receiver decides to go down the line. No matter what the receiver does, though, the poacher should continue moving across to end up in the opposite half of the court.

9 **Talk with your partner.** Doubles teams have got to communicate if they hope to play like a team. And that means talking with each other between points. You should encourage one another, but be careful about giving advice that might seem gratuitous if your partner's game is falling apart.

The most useful exchanges occur when you tell your partner what you intend to do on the next point. For example, when I played with Hewitt, he would mutter to me as he passed by for his next serve—perhaps telling me to poach on a deep second serve or that he would go down the line on his second shot. That way, I could position myself on the court to take advantage of his actions before he made them.

Conversation strengthens your anticipation and gives you extra confidence for the next point. I'm not in favor of one player acting as a captain unless that player is a real doubles expert. To me, doubles is a game of give and take. A team has to find its own strengths and weaknesses and you can do that by talking to each other before the match, during the games and after it's all over. A sense of humor doesn't hurt, either.

23 BREAKING SERVE IN DOUBLES

1 **Get aggressive.** When you receive in doubles, you have a simple objective—to break your opponent's serve. A good doubles team should be able to hold serve against opponents of comparable ability; thus, you need to break your opponents' serve only once to win a set and perhaps only twice to win a match. (I just wish every doubles match I've played could have worked out so easily!) The key to breaking serve is to get aggressive, to take the worthwhile kind of risks that will earn you the points you need. So when you receive, don't be content merely to keep the ball in play. Work with your partner to set up winning situations. Let's look at the best ways to do that.

2 **Return serve crosscourt to the alley.** To win any points as a receiver, you have to develop a reliable return of serve which you can count on against an aggressive server. For my money, the safest return of serve is crosscourt where you have the most court to hit into and the greatest margin of safety since you're hitting the ball over the lowest part of the net. But that's not to say the crosscourt return has to be a defensive shot. Far from it. When you are facing a server who invariably follows his serve to the net, aim your return over to the alley (see the diagram on the far left). The server will be pulled wide and the ball will arrive low to his feet as he runs in. The chances are that the server will be forced to hit a weak half-volley from around shoelace height. And if he does, you or your partner may be able to put the ball away and end the point right there.

3 **Go down the line to keep the net man honest.** Of course, if a receiver always returns crosscourt, the serving team will quickly recognize the pattern and move to counter it. The server's partner can simply begin poaching—moving over to intercept returns and knock them off for winners. So you should mix up your returns by going down the line occasionally (see the diagram on the near right).

The down-the-line return is tougher than the crosscourt return because you have less court to hit into and because you're hitting over the higher, outside part of the net. But if the net man is planning to poach on a crosscourt return, a shot down the line will probably be successful since it will catch him going the wrong way. The occasional down-the-line shot will help your crosscourt returns, too, since the net man will then be cautious about edging over in anticipation of a poach.

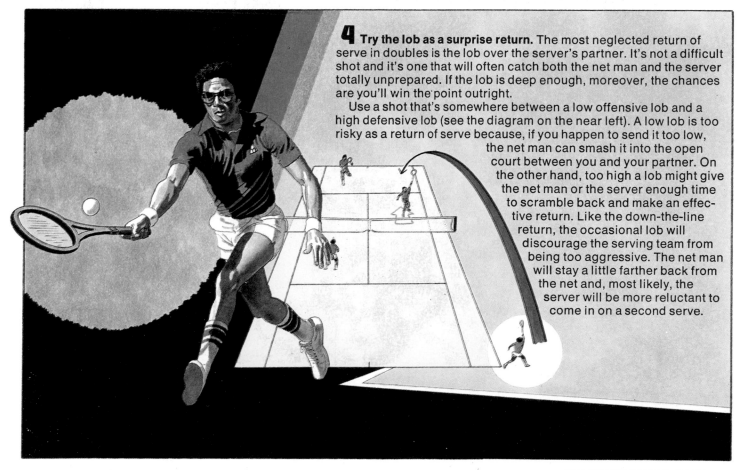

4 **Try the lob as a surprise return.** The most neglected return of serve in doubles is the lob over the server's partner. It's not a difficult shot and it's one that will often catch both the net man and the server totally unprepared. If the lob is deep enough, moreover, the chances are you'll win the point outright.

Use a shot that's somewhere between a low offensive lob and a high defensive lob (see the diagram on the near left). A low lob is too risky as a return of serve because, if you happen to send it too low, the net man can smash it into the open court between you and your partner. On the other hand, too high a lob might give the net man or the server enough time to scramble back and make an effective return. Like the down-the-line return, the occasional lob will discourage the serving team from being too aggressive. The net man will stay a little farther back from the net and, most likely, the server will be more reluctant to come in on a second serve.

5 **Take the net whenever you can.** Doubles is a game that is usually won or lost at the net. So even when you are receiving, you should try to get up to the net to finish off the point. When your partner is receiving serve, you should stand just inside the service box, ready to move up when your partner begins to advance toward the net. When you are receiving, of course, you will be close to the baseline so you'll have to pick your opportunity to go to the net rather carefully.

Don't hesitate to take that chance. For example, be ready to go for the net whenever you force your opponents to hit up (right). Even if the other team is at the net, volleying up will give you a chance to close in, hit down on the ball and probably win the point.

6 **Keep your opponents guessing.** When you're the receiver's partner, your job as I see it is to make life as difficult as possible—within the rules, of course—for the other guys. You should play the way former pro basketball star Bill Bradley did: always be in motion. As soon as the server hits the ball, start moving to get into position to cover the court properly and to distract your opponents a bit.

I'm not suggesting that you shout or stamp your feet, but it's perfectly legal to throw a fake as though you might be thinking of a poach. Such a move could force a down-the-line shot from your opponent, which you could pick off easily at the net. But anything you can do to confuse your opponents is going to help win the point. Never get into the rut, for example, of making the same move each time your partner has to return a wide serve.

7 **Stay in touch with your partner.** When your partner is receiving serve, you should have a pretty good idea of what he aims to do. Between points, talk to each other so that you know what your partner is most likely to do with his return—especially if he intends to do something unusual, like lobbing off a wide serve.

If you are closest to the net, make your moves and let your partner behind you adjust accordingly. After all, your partner can see you, the ball and the other players whereas, unless you have eyes in the back of your head, you can see only the ball and the other team. But good communication should solve that problem ahead of time.

8 Work as a team. It's sometimes difficult for a good singles player to adapt to doubles because he or she has problems sharing the court and the responsibility with another player. For example, many doubles points call for one player to set up a situation where the partner can move in and hit the winning shot with a spectacular volley or overhead. That player, in the spectators' eyes, gets the credit for winning the point and, yet, he or she couldn't have done it unless the situation had been set up by the partner. Stan Smith (left) is a fine example of a player who understands the need for this kind of teamwork in doubles. Although Stan usually plays with Bob Lutz, I've enjoyed the few chances I've had to partner Stan because he has an instinctive feeling for the teamwork needed to win. There's a lot of pleasure to be gained from working as a team—not the least of which is winning the match.

9 Hit with authority. When you're trying to break serve and the chance comes to close out a point, you or your partner should swing firmly and confidently. Step out and punch that volley aggressively or crack that overhead cleanly.

There's a little psychology involved here, too. If you put away the ball with a powerful volley, it will boost your confidence for the next point. And, of course, it can't help but damage your opponents' spirits; they may well become more cautious, particularly when it comes to a critical point—say, 30-40. So keep your strokes and your strategy sharp to break serve.

MIXED DOUBLES CAN BE FUN

1 **The most social form of tennis.** I think we tend to forget that tennis is a very social game, a game that can be played for the sheer pleasure of hitting a ball outdoors on a bright, sunny day with a group of people who simply enjoy each other's company. That's especially true of mixed doubles because it's one of those rare versions of a sport where men and women can compete together, often on equal terms. So although the pros rarely compete in mixed doubles, particularly nowadays with the separate men's and women's tours, I'm very pleased to see that mixed doubles is strong at the club level. That's as it should be because mixed doubles is the fun version of tennis. I'd like to show you how to make mixed doubles even more enjoyable for you and your partner.

2 **Choose your partner carefully.** I really think in mixed doubles you should choose your partner extremely carefully—particularly if you are married and you and your spouse both play tennis. Clearly, it's best if husband and wife play together unless they are truly incompatible on the court. Although my wife Jeanne (right) and I play different styles of tennis, we enjoy mixed doubles together because we have a simple rule that helps us to be compatible partners: I am not allowed to put a ball away, just to keep it in play. That rule makes for some fun tennis we can both enjoy.

If you are choosing a partner who is not your spouse, then the same guidelines apply as to a regular doubles partner. Look for someone whose game will complement yours, who will play well as part of a team and with whom you get on well both on and off the court.

3 **Work together as a team.**
In mixed doubles, the players are often of widely differing abilities and may be inhibited about playing with or against each other. In a situation like that, you and your partner should try to complement each other to make the best of your abilities. For example, when I play with Jeanne and she is serving to a man with a strong crosscourt return of serve, we try to blunt that strength by forcing him to hit his return down the middle where I can get to it with my backhand or Jeanne can take it on her stronger forehand.

Immediately after Jeanne serves (near right), she'll quickly move a few steps toward her alley to open up a hole down the middle quite deliberately. The receiver then will usually go more down the middle where I can move in and handle the ball with comparative ease. That not only enables us to stay in the point but gives us a bonus in that when Jeanne is confident of her ability to handle the return of serve, she becomes more confident of her serve, too, and hits the ball more aggressively

4 **Go for consistency.**
As with regular doubles, you'll win at mixed doubles play by making fewer errors. That means going for consistency instead of outright winners. If your best return of serve, for example, is crosscourt, use it even if that means returning to the stronger player. To get the consistency you want, it helps to give yourself a little extra time by standing deeper behind the baseline. I've noticed, for instance, that women club players often don't hit as deep as their male counterparts and so they stand inside the baseline to receive serve or during a rally. If you have that habit, standing deeper behind the baseline will give you more time to hit your shot and help you to be more consistent. And moving forward is much easier than backpedaling in a hurry.

5 **Be adventurous.** Mixed doubles may be your chance to experiment, play a different game and have lots of fun doing it. If you are playing with an aggressive partner who likes to go to the net, why not do it? When Jeanne and I play together, I encourage her to go to the net. To be sure, we don't win every point that way, but she gets a kick out of it and the experience helps her to be more aggressive in regular doubles and singles play.

If you are the stronger player, remember not to hog all the action. Give your partner a chance to try something new and give her (or him) all the encouragement you can. But do it without being domineering. If your partner blows a point, chalk it up to experience and don't become exasperated. That way, mixed doubles will be fun for both of you.

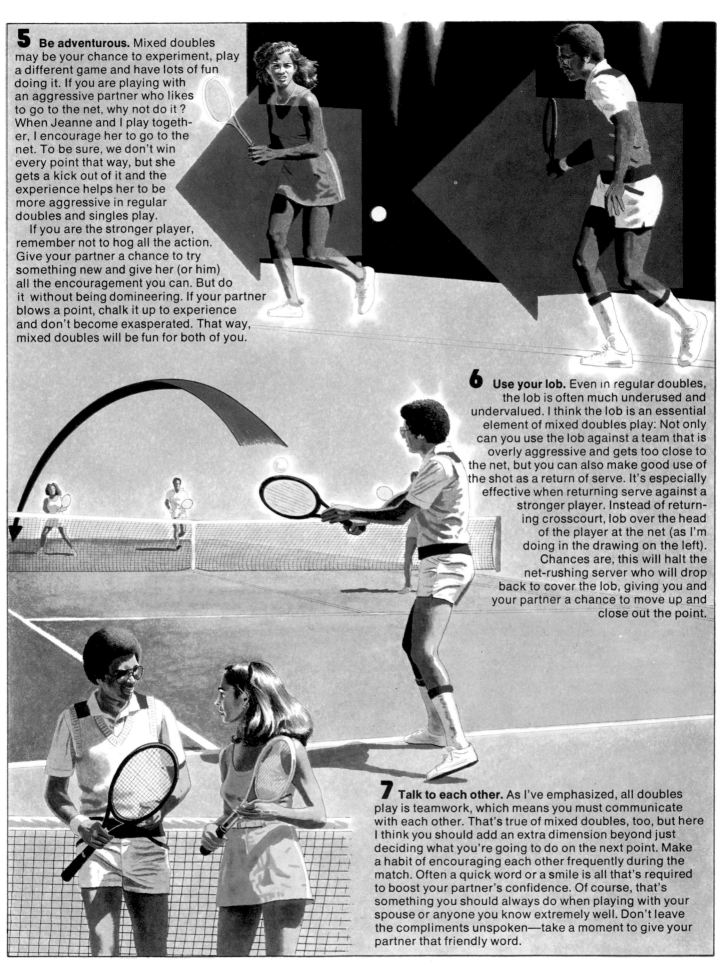

6 **Use your lob.** Even in regular doubles, the lob is often much underused and undervalued. I think the lob is an essential element of mixed doubles play. Not only can you use the lob against a team that is overly aggressive and gets too close to the net, but you can also make good use of the shot as a return of serve. It's especially effective when returning serve against a stronger player. Instead of returning crosscourt, lob over the head of the player at the net (as I'm doing in the drawing on the left). Chances are, this will halt the net-rushing server who will drop back to cover the lob, giving you and your partner a chance to move up and close out the point.

7 **Talk to each other.** As I've emphasized, all doubles play is teamwork, which means you must communicate with each other. That's true of mixed doubles, too, but here I think you should add an extra dimension beyond just deciding what you're going to do on the next point. Make a habit of encouraging each other frequently during the match. Often a quick word or a smile is all that's required to boost your partner's confidence. Of course, that's something you should always do when playing with your spouse or anyone you know extremely well. Don't leave the compliments unspoken—take a moment to give your partner that friendly word.

8 **Make the best of your partner's abilities.** Success in mixed doubles comes to those teams who make the best use of their abilities. Nowhere is this more true than in the pro ranks where the successful mixed doubles teams are often players with relatively undistinguished singles records. For example, Bob Hewitt and Greer Stevens are one of the best mixed doubles teams I've ever seen. Hewitt has great doubles court sense, and although he's not a flashy player he has one of the best returns of serve in the business. Bob is probably one of the top doubles players of all time. Greer complements him perfectly because she's a steady player. Their opponents often try to hit away from Bob but Greer simply moves over to hit that great forehand topspin of hers, which she can do all day long. The two of them make an almost unbeatable pair because their abilities are so complementary.

9 **Mixed doubles is only a game.** I think the male approach to mixed doubles is often flawed because the man wants to demonstrate his superiority over the woman on court. I've often seen situations where the man can hit the ball harder than his partner but she is simply a better doubles player. Doubles really is a game where craft and skill can outwit sheer power. When the teams are mixed, there's no reason why a woman cannot outplay a man at the club level. When that happens, it's time for the male ego to take a back seat.

Similarly, the guy who is a dominant player should resist the temptation to put his partner on one side and to cover all the court himself. I'm reminded of basketball players who are so good that they get double-teamed. A player like that may score a lot of points, but unless he passes the ball off, he'll soon get tired, begin to make mistakes, and his team will lose. So it often is with the macho guy in tennis who tries to do it all. He ends up being on the losing team. Make mixed doubles a social game that two men and two women can enjoy together and you'll have one of the most rewarding of all sports.

PART VI
TRAINING AND EQUIPMENT

25 A LESSON IN TAKING LESSONS

1 **The importance of instruction.** Every player—from the novice to the nationally-ranked professional—can profit from the right kind of instruction. It's especially important, of course, when a person is starting out in the sport since tennis is an acquired skill, not an instinctive one. But it's also vital for players to continue to take lessons from time to time as they advance through the intermediate and advanced levels of the sport. Otherwise, they're likely to find their games stagnating and to develop bad habits that will go uncorrected. So here, I'd like to offer a few pointers—based on my own experiences as a player and a teacher—that will help you arrive at the best teaching program for you.

2 **How to pick a teaching professional.** It's as tough to choose a good tennis teacher as it is to pick a good doctor or car mechanic. Personal recommendation counts for a lot, but I think you should begin by looking at pros who have become certified teachers either as members of the U.S. Professional Tennis Association or the Professional Tennis Registry. Then, watch the pro give a lesson and see how he or she handles the students. Can you see any improvement? Does the pro seem to understand individual problems? Above all, are the students enjoying the lesson? When you think you've located a good pro, take a sample lesson. If the lesson works for you, go ahead and sign up for regular lessons or clinics with that pro.

3 **The advantages of the private lesson.** If you are not an absolute beginner who has never hit a tennis ball, I think private individual lessons are probably best for you. You'll get more personal attention, you'll hit more balls and you'll be spared the embarrassment of performing in front of a group. Of course, private lessons can be expensive; but a weekly half-hour lesson that costs $15 or $20 isn't a lot when you consider that the good habits a fine teacher will impart should stay with you for a lifetime of tennis enjoyment. But see to it that you get your money's worth from a private lesson: 1) Tell the pro what you'd like to work on each time and, 2) make sure that he works you hard.

4 Getting the most from a group clinic.

A group lesson can be really valuable—if the instructor is good and the group is small. I've found that a group lesson is most successful if it's limited to no more than four or five students; that way, everyone gets a chance to hit even when I'm working with one particular student. In the clinics that I give at the Doral Country Club in Miami, I start out by demonstrating the strokes to all the participants. But then we divide them into small groups, each with a teaching pro, for close individual attention. When you take part in a group lesson, stay alert all the time—even when the pro is working with other students. You can often learn from other's mistakes. And try to enroll with some friends so you can practice after the lesson.

5 Consider a tennis camp.

If you are interested in using your vacation time to improve your tennis, a tennis camp or clinic is the perfect answer. You'll be with a group of guests who are all tennis players, so you'll all have something in common right away. Most of the better adult camps and clinics, moreover, offer some sort of off-court social programs, making the conditions right for everyone to have a good time—and learn some tennis, too. But remember that playing tennis for several hours every day, often in the hot sun, can be punishing if you're not prepared for it.

6 **Practice what you've learned.** Your game won't improve if you simply take a lesson and then head off to join your regular weekly group. You must really work to get the instructor's tips so ingrained that they become instinctive. So immediately after a lesson, line up another player, if you possibly can, and practice the points that you've just learned from the pro. The two of you can do the same drills that he or she used. Even those of us who play professionally practice for several hours a day, often concentrating on one particular stroke for 15 minutes or a half hour. You and your practice partner can help each other out by feeding balls or by working on complementary shots—like the lob and overhead.

7 **Chart your progress as you improve.** Every couple of months or so, you should monitor your tennis progress by having a friend chart one of your matches. Your friend should note how each point was won or lost and with which stroke. You can easily make up a chart listing forehand winners and errors, volley winners and errors, and so on (see right). After the match, add up your various winners and errors to see the strengths and weaknesses in your game. It's a good idea to discuss the results with your teaching pro so he can tailor your future lessons to them. Chart some matches at regular intervals to see how your game is improving.

PLAYER: MIKE SMITH		OPPONENT: JOHN JONES		DATE	
STROKE		CROSSCOURT	TOTALS	DOWN THE LINE	TOTAL
FORE-HAND	W	IIII IIII I	11	IIII III	8
	E	IIII IIII IIII II	17	IIII IIII IIII	15
BACK-HAND	W	IIII IIII	10	IIII III	8
	E	IIII			
RETURN OF SERVE	W	IIII			
	E	IIII			
FORE-HAND VOLLEY	W	IIII			
	E	IIII			
BACK-HAND VOLLEY	W	IIII			
	E	IIII			
SMASH	W				

8 **Take a refresher lesson to stop bad habits.** Even when you can play a pretty good game of tennis, it pays to take an occasional lesson from an expert teaching pro. Let the pro put you through your repertoire of strokes so he can note any bad habits that may have crept into your game and show you how to get rid of them. You may need a couple of lessons to get straightened out again. Of course, you should check with the pro promptly when you feel that part of your game is becoming a problem. It's easy to recognize your own deficiencies, but it's not always so simple to correct them by yourself. Or maybe your strokes are sound but you can't seem to beat players you feel you should. In that case, ask the pro to watch you play a match. He ought to be able to spot your problem.

9 **Teaching a child.** If your child expresses an interest in tennis, you should encourage him or her to take lessons right from the start. It will be an investment in a sport the child can enjoy for a lifetime. But it's especially important that children take lessons from a teaching pro who enjoys teaching kids and has been successful at it. Nothing will turn a child off tennis faster than a poor teacher. With children, it's even more vital to make the game fun than it is with adults because tennis can be frustrating for a youngster. The pro has to be able to recognize these frustrations and head them off quickly. If your child shows signs of developing into a competitive player, you might consider one of the top children's tennis camps listed in the January issue of TENNIS. However, never push your child in tennis. Let the youngster go at his own pace.

10 **Advanced coaching.** If you become a truly strong player—perhaps good enough to get a local or national ranking—you may find that you still require help but have a hard time getting it from your local pro. There's nothing surprising about that; many tennis pros are fine teachers of beginning and intermediate players, but they may lack the skill and experience necessary to coach an advanced player. My advice is to find a coach who has played at your level or above. Even pros will go to a Pancho Segura or a Dennis Ralston to iron out the kinks in their games. I remember Segura telling me some years ago that I should lob more to throw my opponents off balance. I tried it and he was right. You may be able to find an older, formerly-ranked player who can help you or a college coach who gives the occasional private lesson. If you are a promising young player, coaches may come to you and offer their services.

1 Why you should practice. Playing tennis is such fun that many players seem reluctant to spend time practicing it. That's a mistake, of course, because practice is the best way to use your court time if you're serious about raising the level of your game. In a properly organized practice session, you'll hit many more balls than you would in a couple of sets of match play. In fact, do you know who practices the most? Tennis professionals. The pros know that you have to work to keep your game at a high level. And practice doesn't have to be a drag, as I hope to show you.

2 Write down your strengths and weaknesses. First of all, let's get organized. Take out a sheet of paper, write down your strengths on one side and your weaknesses on the other. These lists will tell you where to put your priorities when you practice. If your backhand lob is bad news, spend five or 10 minutes of your practice session working on it; your partner can return the lobs with overhead smashes so you'll both benefit. However, don't forget to write down your strengths, too. You should begin your practice with the strokes you can hit well to warm up and to get your timing down.

3 Warm up before you practice. If you practice properly, you'll be working hard—perhaps even harder than you do in a match. That's because you'll hit more balls and probably do more running to keep the ball in play than you would in competition. So you should warm up carefully before your practice session. Start with some easy stretching exercises. I like to begin by loosening my neck muscles, then my arms, upper body and legs until I've stretched just about every muscle that I could possibly use when playing. Make sure you are physically warm before you start hitting balls. That's especially important in the cooler months, but I make it a rule to warm up every time I go out on the court. So should you.

4 **Start out slowly.** After stretching exercises, begin your on-court practice by hitting easy balls for a few minutes. If you and your partner have good forehands, hit some forehands to each other. But don't demonstrate your prowess by hitting winners; simply try to keep a rally going. As you warm up, gradually increase the depth and pace of your balls and begin hitting to both sides. Start to hit wider balls so you both have to run to make your returns. When you are hitting easily, move up to the net and hit a few volleys. Get your partner to hit some easy balls, then some low ones and some wide ones. Then, do the same for him. Finally, finish off with a few unhurried serves and some lobs that can be smashed without difficulty. Do it all at a relatively slow pace so you get thoroughly warm and can hit with consistency and confidence. After that, you can get down to the real business of practicing.

5 **Practice as you would play.** I think the best way to make practice as exciting as a real match is to practice a shot in what I call its "natural setting." For example, if I want to practice serving, I don't just take a basket of balls and hit one serve after another. I serve and then follow the ball to the net so my practice partner and I can play out the point. That way, I get to work on my serve and volley, which is the natural game for me (except on slow clay courts, of course), and my partner gets to work on his return of serve. In the same way, if I want to work on my volleys, I'll start from the service line and then try to make my way to the net while my partner is trying to hit passing shots or even attempting to lob over my head. To make things even more interesting, you can keep score during these game-like practice routines.

6 **Work on your weaknesses.** When you are well into your practice session, that's the time to bring out your list of weaknesses and get really serious. Spend 10 minutes on a single problem shot. You'll be amazed by the number of balls you can hit in 10 minutes. And you'll be equally surprised, I'll bet, by the improvement in your shot after that amount of concentrated hitting. Suppose low volleys give you trouble. Stand back on the service line and have your practice partner send balls to you low over the net. Hit every ball before it bounces, but move back to the service line after each one. That way, almost all the balls you get will be low volleys. You're rarely going to win the point with a low volley, so just concentrate on getting the ball over the net.

7 **Work out with two-on-one drills.** If you can find two practice partners, try a two-on-one drill. It will be a great workout for all and a lot of fun in the bargain. These drills are the kind favored by the famous former Australian Davis Cup coach, Harry Hopman, and are often called Australian drills. You can either put one player at the net and two players on the baseline (upper drawing) or one player on the baseline and two players at the net (lower drawing). The key to these drills is consistency. The three of you should try to keep the ball in play in order to hit the most balls in the shortest period of time. Of course, the two players at the net should try to make the baseliner run from side to side, but they should not close out the point, although I guarantee that the temptation will be awfully strong. Similarly, the two baseliners should resist the temptation to zip a passing shot down the line out of reach of the net man. Your job is to keep the ball in play, making as few errors as possible and yet extending yourself as much as you can.

8 **Improve your control with half-court tennis.** Success in tennis depends so much on finesse and control that you should work on those qualities, too, when you practice. To do that, I like to play a version of half-court tennis in which my practice partner and I use one half of the court length-wise. One player starts at the net and has to hit volleys that go deeper than the service line but still within half the court. The player on the baseline tries to force his partner away from the net by using lobs and passing shots. If the net player loses a point, he retreats to the baseline and the positions are reversed.

9 **Extend yourself when you practice.** While I've stressed the importance of consistency when you practice, I don't want you to get the idea that you should be conservative. Your practice sessions should also be a time to experiment, to try the difficult or to develop a new shot. In short, you should extend yourself as you practice. For example, even if your partner's lob is going out, smash it back by making that extra effort. Similarly, get your partner to blast a few cannonball serves at you and try to return any that clear the net, even if they land outside the service box. The next time you face a hard serve in a match, you'll have that shorter blocking swing all grooved and ready for action. And when your strokes feel good in practice, make life a little tougher by taking the ball earlier. By extending yourself as you practice, you'll realize that you can do more than you'd thought possible. That's a major benefit of practice.

27 KEEPING FIT TO PLAY BETTER

1 **Why conditioning helps.** Every player, whether a pro or a twice-a-week enthusiast, needs a proper exercise program to play his or her best tennis. It will strengthen your muscles, build your stamina and, combined with a few warm-up routines before matches, greatly reduce the chance of muscular injury. And, of course, by keeping fit you'll improve your general health and, more than likely, reduce your weight by a few pounds. If you intend to run around a tennis court on the weekend, you'll be surprised how much easier that is when you've shed some excess poundage.

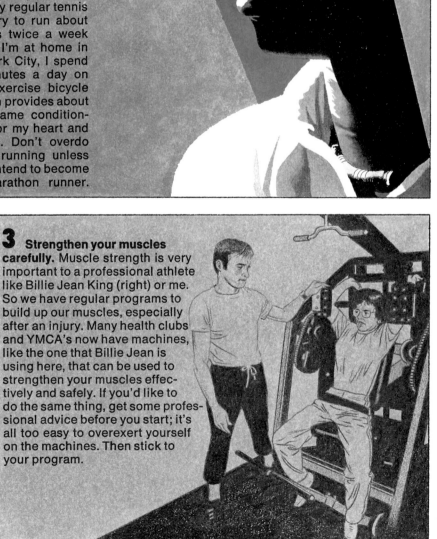

2 **Run to build your stamina.** To get and keep fit, the first thing you must do is increase the capacity of your heart and lungs—what the doctors call your cardiovascular capacity. You can do that by running a few miles every day. Get a checkup from your physician before you start and take his advice on how much you should do. Besides my regular tennis practice, I try to run about three miles twice a week or, when I'm at home in New York City, I spend 20 minutes a day on my exercise bicycle which provides about the same conditioning for my heart and lungs. Don't overdo your running unless you intend to become a marathon runner.

3 **Strengthen your muscles carefully.** Muscle strength is very important to a professional athlete like Billie Jean King (right) or me. So we have regular programs to build up our muscles, especially after an injury. Many health clubs and YMCA's now have machines, like the one that Billie Jean is using here, that can be used to strengthen your muscles effectively and safely. If you'd like to do the same thing, get some professional advice before you start; it's all too easy to overexert yourself on the machines. Then stick to your program.

4 **Stretching for warm-up and general fitness.** Before you go out to play, it's vital that you run through a set of warm-up exercises to stretch your muscles—as John Newcombe is doing here. On this and the following page, I'm going to show you the warm-up and stretching exercises that I do myself. You can use these routines in two ways: for a warm-up of five minutes or so before you play, or for a longer daily program on those days when you do not play tennis.

5 **Loosen your neck and shoulders.** I like to think of stretching as something you should do from head to toe, so I recommend that you start with your neck and shoulders. For the neck, stand with your feet shoulder-width apart, hands on your hips, and just roll your head around your shoulders as forcefully and slowly as you can (right). When the creaking subsides, you've loosened up your neck. Then, you should roll your shoulders forward in a circle. Do that 10 times and then reverse direction.

6 **Unlimber your body.** Now, we move to a couple of routines to stretch the upper body. First, stand with your feet a little more than shoulder-width apart, arms held out horizontally (left). Just swing your body around keeping your feet firmly planted on the ground. Do it gently at first, but each time you swing, try to go around a little further. Do this exercise maybe 10 or 15 times. Next, stand with your feet shoulder-width apart and dangle your arms loosely by your sides. Now, swing your arms up and around in as wide a circular arc as possible. Do it 10 times and then reverse direction. Your back and shoulder muscles should be quite loose by now.

7 **Stretch your stomach and legs.** These exercises are a little more strenuous than the preceding set, so you should take care not to overdo things when you start out. Begin by standing with your legs spread as wide apart as you can manage to get them, and rest your hands on your thighs. Lean to one side (left), sliding your hand down your leg. Then, lean to the other side, and keep alternating sides. Go gently at first, but try to lean a little farther each time. After 10 repetitions or so, reach down with your right hand to touch your right foot and slowly draw an arc from your right to your left foot and back again. Do the same thing alternately with your left hand.

8 **Build up your legs.** Toe touches are excellent for strengthening your leg muscles. Stand with your legs shoulder-width apart and bend over as far as you can —without bouncing or straining your back. Hold the position for five seconds and then come up again. Try to go down a little farther next time but don't push it too far. When I first started this exercise, I couldn't touch my toes at all, but now I'm so flexible that I can put my nose between my knees. Doing that will take you a long time, I can assure you.

9 **Strengthen your knees by jumping.** This exercise is an excellent way to finish off your warm-up because it will really get the blood flowing and make you feel ready to start playing. Just stand in place and jump up in the air as high as you can. Bend your knees to get as much spring into your jump as possible. Let your hands go high above your head so that your entire body is part of the exercise. Ten times should be enough. Five minutes of these last five exercises should be enough to get you thoroughly warmed up and set to play.

10 **Speed up your footwork.** Tennis is a game that calls for short, rapid movements around the court. So I suggest that you add a couple of footwork drills to the other conditioning routines I've described. These drills were developed by Dennis Ralston when he was the U.S. Davis Cup coach. For the first drill, stand at the back fence, run up and touch the baseline and then, without turning around, back up to the fence. Next time, run from the back fence to the service line and back up. Then, sprint from the fence to the net and back up.

11 **Improve your sideways mobility.** Stand at the center mark on the baseline while a practice partner stands at the "T" of the service line with two balls. Your partner then rolls a ball to you to one side of the court, forcing you to skip along the baseline to intercept it. You must move, get down, stop the ball and roll it right back. Meanwhile, your partner should roll the second ball toward the other side of the court so that you have to skip back smartly to intercept that ball and return it. This exercise can continue until you protest loudly enough.

12 **Get started now.** I recognize that, for a lot of players, conditioning is like reading a classic or taking a physical: they know it would be good for them, but it doesn't sound like fun, so they put it off. That's a shame, because it's so easy to work yourself into an exercise routine and because the benefits are so great. Start slowly and build up to a level of fitness that you can maintain with some running or bicycling, plus a few minutes of stretching exercises every day. You'll soon begin to see a significant improvement in your game. For me, that's reason enough to get fit and stay that way.

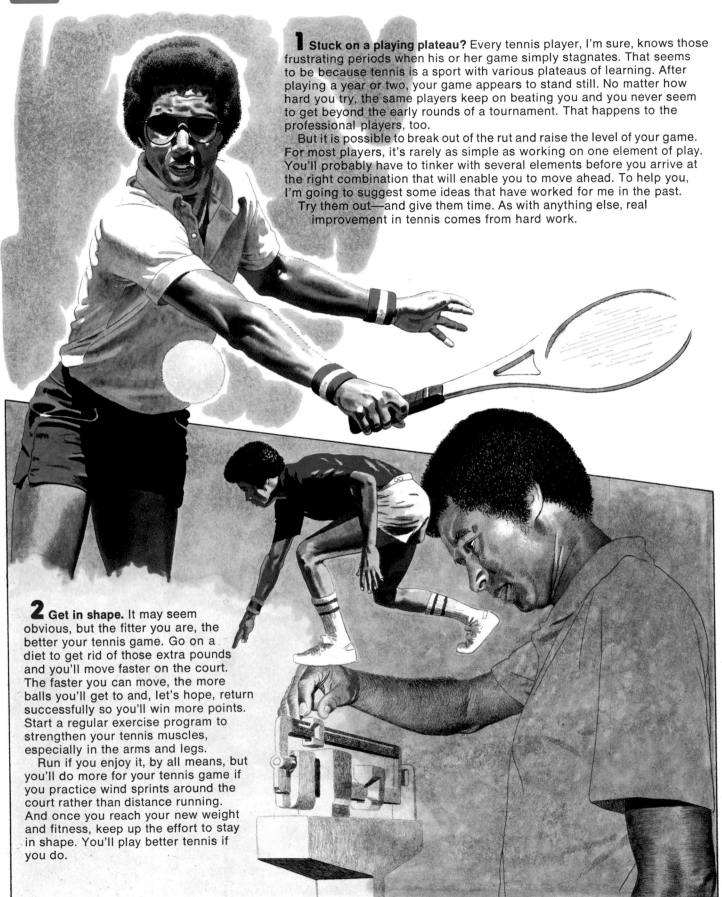

1 **Stuck on a playing plateau?** Every tennis player, I'm sure, knows those frustrating periods when his or her game simply stagnates. That seems to be because tennis is a sport with various plateaus of learning. After playing a year or two, your game appears to stand still. No matter how hard you try, the same players keep on beating you and you never seem to get beyond the early rounds of a tournament. That happens to the professional players, too.

But it is possible to break out of the rut and raise the level of your game. For most players, it's rarely as simple as working on one element of play. You'll probably have to tinker with several elements before you arrive at the right combination that will enable you to move ahead. To help you, I'm going to suggest some ideas that have worked for me in the past.

Try them out—and give them time. As with anything else, real improvement in tennis comes from hard work.

2 **Get in shape.** It may seem obvious, but the fitter you are, the better your tennis game. Go on a diet to get rid of those extra pounds and you'll move faster on the court. The faster you can move, the more balls you'll get to and, let's hope, return successfully so you'll win more points. Start a regular exercise program to strengthen your tennis muscles, especially in the arms and legs.

Run if you enjoy it, by all means, but you'll do more for your tennis game if you practice wind sprints around the court rather than distance running. And once you reach your new weight and fitness, keep up the effort to stay in shape. You'll play better tennis if you do.

3 **Seek help for your strokes.** Just as a car needs a regular tune-up to run well, your game needs a periodic overhaul by a good teaching pro. Every six months or so, go back to a pro who knows your game well. The chances are that you'll have developed a few bad habits he'll spot right away. If it takes a few lessons to correct those flaws and put some extra polish on your strokes, it's worth the investment.

Throughout my playing career, I never hesitated to go to experts like Pancho Gonzalez (far right) who could see my problems more clearly than I could myself. Gonzalez had seen me play many times over the years, so he could point out subtle changes in my grip or serving motion that had crept in without my noticing. A pro who knows your game can do the same for you.

4 **Learn a new shot.** When you go back to your pro for your tune-up, ask him to start you working on a new stroke. For example, if you are a competent intermediate player, perhaps you'd like to try the topspin lob. That's not a stroke you'll hit very often. But it's one that can come in handy; and the knowledge that you can hit it will often give you a psychological boost.

Players who have beaten you in the past will be surprised when you pull your new shot on them. Raising the level of your game is sometimes a question of a mental block. Trying something new can be an excellent way to help remove that block.

5 **Change your equipment.** Nothing seems to boost a player's confidence—and court performance—quite so dramatically as a brand new racquet. Perhaps you've had the experience of playing surprisingly well with a new racquet. That improvement usually falls off a bit as you become used to the new model. Nonetheless, a new racquet, or even a new stringing job, may be enough to add an extra edge to your game. And playing with different racquets can be an entertaining exercise that will take your mind off your stagnating game.

6 **Have a friend chart your game.** Many club players can hit the ball well but don't seem to win many matches. In those cases, something obviously is lacking and a good way to identify it is to ask a friend to chart one of your matches. Have your friend mark down the result of each point and how it was won or lost. After the match, you can use the totals to determine your strengths and weaknesses under match pressure. You then know the weak strokes that you have to work on to win more points. Few players realize that most points are over after the ball has crossed the net five times. If you can remain error-free through four or five hits, most points will be yours.

7 **Take a playing lesson.** If you are a relatively good player, your strokes may not be the cause of your lack of improvement. Your strategy may be faulty. If that's the case, I recommend you take a playing lesson with a pro or a coach who has had plenty of competitive experience. Play a match with the pro so he can test your strategy and point out your weaknesses.

I've noticed that many club players are indecisive, perhaps because they lack the confidence to do the right thing. A pro may suggest that you hit your approach shots down the line to reduce the available angles for your opponent as you come to the net. Or he may advise you to use high topspin shots to keep your opponent back behind the baseline. A pro can guide you toward the best strategy for your game.

8 **Develop a game plan.** Get into the habit of working out a game plan before you go into a match. To do that in a tournament, it's helpful to watch your next opponent in action and make a few notes about his weaknesses that can become part of your plan. Or ask another player how to play against him.

I've known players who write out game plans and consult them at changeovers. But when you have sufficient experience, it's enough to compile your game plan mentally. Just be sure to do it before you go on court to warm up. It's especially important for you and your doubles partner to have a game plan that you both understand— and agree on— beforehand. Compare your notes on the other team and plan your strategies before the match.

9 **Analyze your opponent during a match.** When you are facing a player who beats you consistently or a new opponent who seems to be outplaying you, try watching him more intently. Does he make more errors on the backhand return of serve? Does he favor the forehand approach? Are there any shots he's afraid to hit?

Incidentally, you can often tell by the look on a player's face which shots he doesn't like to hit. Force him to make those shots and you'll undermine his confidence little by little. If he likes hard-hit shots, for instance, give him plenty of soft, sliced balls that lack pace. Size up your opponent's play in your mind so you can adjust your game plan to counter his.

10 **How to put it all together.** It isn't easy to lift your game from its present plateau. And what works for one player will not necessarily work for another. Yet a simple improvement in one area can lead to improvements elsewhere, with dramatic results for your overall game.

Some time ago, I suggested to Vitas Gerulaitis (right) that he should develop a topspin backhand to complement his hard slice. He did, meanwhile working with his coach, Fred Stolle, to build his game to a point where he would rank as one of the premier players in the world. He succeeded, of course, and that topspin backhand is one of the weapons that enabled him to do it.

I mention that not to claim any credit for Vitas' improvement but as an illustration of what can be done by trying some new approaches and putting in plenty of hard work in practice. You can raise the level of your game by following his example.

29 CHOOSING A RACQUET

1 **The basic decision.** The selection of a racquet is the most important equipment decision that a tennis player makes. But it has to be a personal one since every player is different—with his or her own style of play and personal preferences. All I can do is give you some general guidelines that are intended to help you make an intelligent choice. Racquet design has improved so much lately that it is no longer possible to say that wood racquets are best for one type of player and metal racquets best for another. What can be said, though, is that there is such an enormous range of wood, metal and composite racquets available today that you should, by shopping carefully, be able to find just the one to suit you and your game.

2 **Swing for yourself.** Your first step should be to visit a pro shop or sporting goods store with a wide selection of racquets and heft as many different racquets as you can to see which appeal to you. Hit a few imaginary backhands and forehands—and, maybe, a serve if the ceiling is high enough in the store. When you find a few racquets that you like, ask the pro or store manager if he has demonstrator models that you can borrow for the day to test on the court before you make your final decision. If the store doesn't have demonstrators or won't rent you a racquet, try another store. I would never advise buying a racquet without trying it out first.

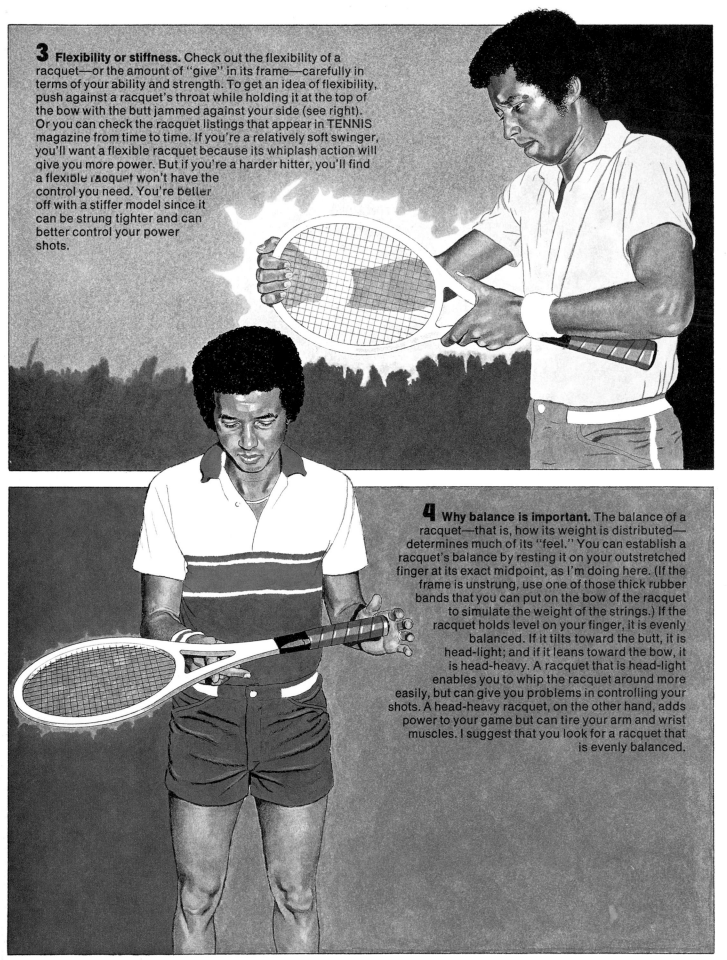

3 **Flexibility or stiffness.** Check out the flexibility of a racquet—or the amount of "give" in its frame—carefully in terms of your ability and strength. To get an idea of flexibility, push against a racquet's throat while holding it at the top of the bow with the butt jammed against your side (see right). Or you can check the racquet listings that appear in TENNIS magazine from time to time. If you're a relatively soft swinger, you'll want a flexible racquet because its whiplash action will give you more power. But if you're a harder hitter, you'll find a flexible racquet won't have the control you need. You're better off with a stiffer model since it can be strung tighter and can better control your power shots.

4 **Why balance is important.** The balance of a racquet—that is, how its weight is distributed—determines much of its "feel." You can establish a racquet's balance by resting it on your outstretched finger at its exact midpoint, as I'm doing here. (If the frame is unstrung, use one of those thick rubber bands that you can put on the bow of the racquet to simulate the weight of the strings.) If the racquet holds level on your finger, it is evenly balanced. If it tilts toward the butt, it is head-light; and if it leans toward the bow, it is head-heavy. A racquet that is head-light enables you to whip the racquet around more easily, but can give you problems in controlling your shots. A head-heavy racquet, on the other hand, adds power to your game but can tire your arm and wrist muscles. I suggest that you look for a racquet that is evenly balanced.

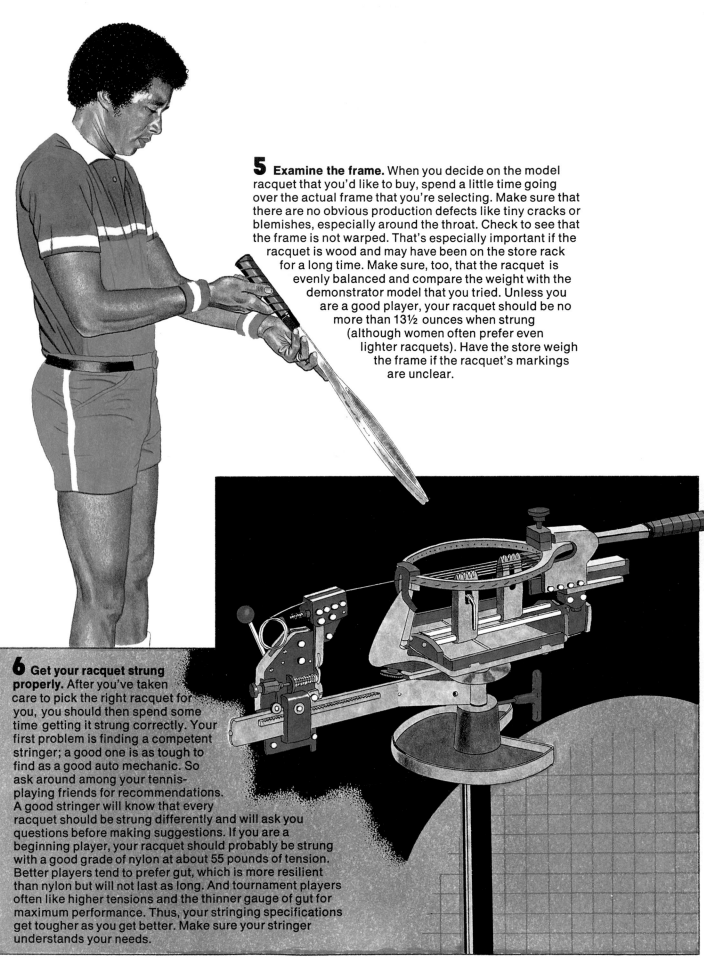

5 **Examine the frame.** When you decide on the model racquet that you'd like to buy, spend a little time going over the actual frame that you're selecting. Make sure that there are no obvious production defects like tiny cracks or blemishes, especially around the throat. Check to see that the frame is not warped. That's especially important if the racquet is wood and may have been on the store rack for a long time. Make sure, too, that the racquet is evenly balanced and compare the weight with the demonstrator model that you tried. Unless you are a good player, your racquet should be no more than 13½ ounces when strung (although women often prefer even lighter racquets). Have the store weigh the frame if the racquet's markings are unclear.

6 **Get your racquet strung properly.** After you've taken care to pick the right racquet for you, you should then spend some time getting it strung correctly. Your first problem is finding a competent stringer; a good one is as tough to find as a good auto mechanic. So ask around among your tennis-playing friends for recommendations. A good stringer will know that every racquet should be strung differently and will ask you questions before making suggestions. If you are a beginning player, your racquet should probably be strung with a good grade of nylon at about 55 pounds of tension. Better players tend to prefer gut, which is more resilient than nylon but will not last as long. And tournament players often like higher tensions and the thinner gauge of gut for maximum performance. Thus, your stringing specifications get tougher as you get better. Make sure your stringer understands your needs.

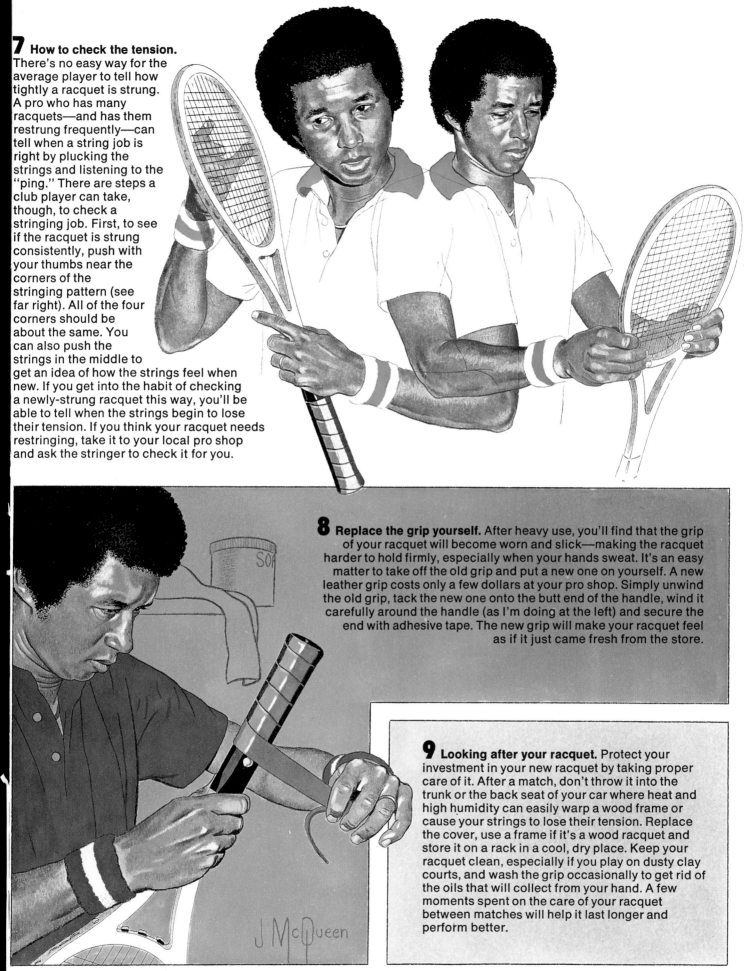

7 **How to check the tension.** There's no easy way for the average player to tell how tightly a racquet is strung. A pro who has many racquets—and has them restrung frequently—can tell when a string job is right by plucking the strings and listening to the "ping." There are steps a club player can take, though, to check a stringing job. First, to see if the racquet is strung consistently, push with your thumbs near the corners of the stringing pattern (see far right). All of the four corners should be about the same. You can also push the strings in the middle to get an idea of how the strings feel when new. If you get into the habit of checking a newly-strung racquet this way, you'll be able to tell when the strings begin to lose their tension. If you think your racquet needs restringing, take it to your local pro shop and ask the stringer to check it for you.

8 **Replace the grip yourself.** After heavy use, you'll find that the grip of your racquet will become worn and slick—making the racquet harder to hold firmly, especially when your hands sweat. It's an easy matter to take off the old grip and put a new one on yourself. A new leather grip costs only a few dollars at your pro shop. Simply unwind the old grip, tack the new one onto the butt end of the handle, wind it carefully around the handle (as I'm doing at the left) and secure the end with adhesive tape. The new grip will make your racquet feel as if it just came fresh from the store.

9 **Looking after your racquet.** Protect your investment in your new racquet by taking proper care of it. After a match, don't throw it into the trunk or the back seat of your car where heat and high humidity can easily warp a wood frame or cause your strings to lose their tension. Replace the cover, use a frame if it's a wood racquet and store it on a rack in a cool, dry place. Keep your racquet clean, especially if you play on dusty clay courts, and wash the grip occasionally to get rid of the oils that will collect from your hand. A few moments spent on the care of your racquet between matches will help it last longer and perform better.

30 GEARING UP

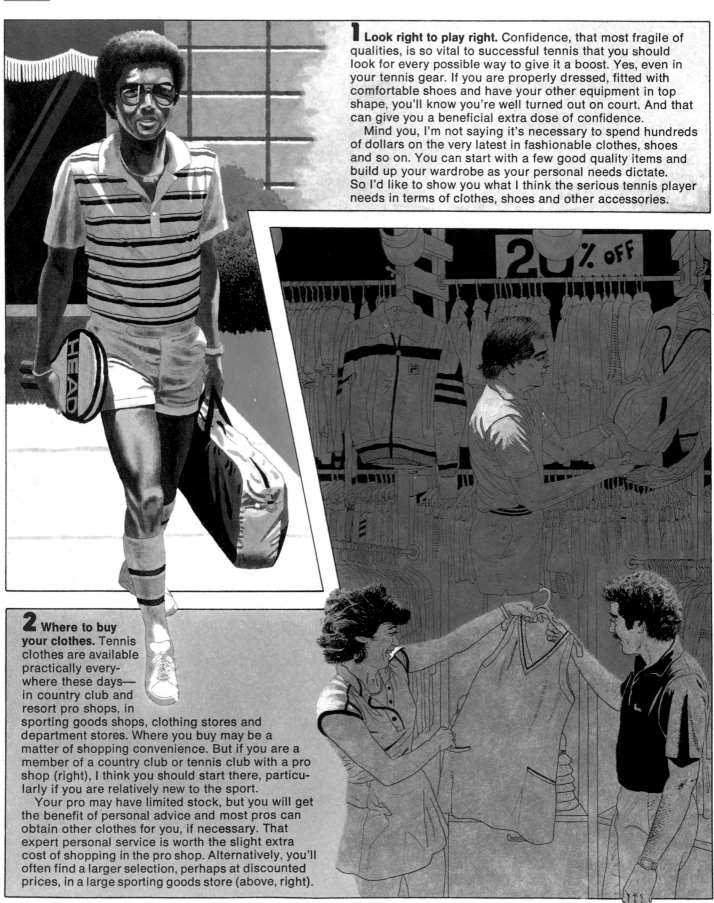

1 Look right to play right. Confidence, that most fragile of qualities, is so vital to successful tennis that you should look for every possible way to give it a boost. Yes, even in your tennis gear. If you are properly dressed, fitted with comfortable shoes and have your other equipment in top shape, you'll know you're well turned out on court. And that can give you a beneficial extra dose of confidence.

Mind you, I'm not saying it's necessary to spend hundreds of dollars on the very latest in fashionable clothes, shoes and so on. You can start with a few good quality items and build up your wardrobe as your personal needs dictate. So I'd like to show you what I think the serious tennis player needs in terms of clothes, shoes and other accessories.

2 Where to buy your clothes. Tennis clothes are available practically everywhere these days—in country club and resort pro shops, in sporting goods shops, clothing stores and department stores. Where you buy may be a matter of shopping convenience. But if you are a member of a country club or tennis club with a pro shop (right), I think you should start there, particularly if you are relatively new to the sport.

Your pro may have limited stock, but you will get the benefit of personal advice and most pros can obtain other clothes for you, if necessary. That expert personal service is worth the slight extra cost of shopping in the pro shop. Alternatively, you'll often find a larger selection, perhaps at discounted prices, in a large sporting goods store (above, right).

3 **Your basic tennis wardrobe.** Spread out on the table are items that I consider necessary for the serious tennis player. You can play tennis with fewer clothes and, of course, you can make your tennis wardrobe as large as your pocketbook will permit. But with these outfits, you'll be sure that you'll always have the clothes to meet any match situation year-round. My suggestions are for a male wardrobe, but a woman can substitute tennis dresses for the shorts and shirts. The rest of the wardrobe will do for both sexes.

I recommend three sets of shirts and shorts (or three dresses for women) so that you'll always have a freshly laundered outfit every time you go out to play. Long and short-sleeved sweaters are useful for the year-round player and so, too, is a warm-up suit. I think you should have at least two pairs of shoes so you'll have a dry pair ready when you play on successive days. And you can never have too many tennis socks. Finally, I advise a visor or sun hat, wrist and sweat bands plus a bag for all your gear and racquets.

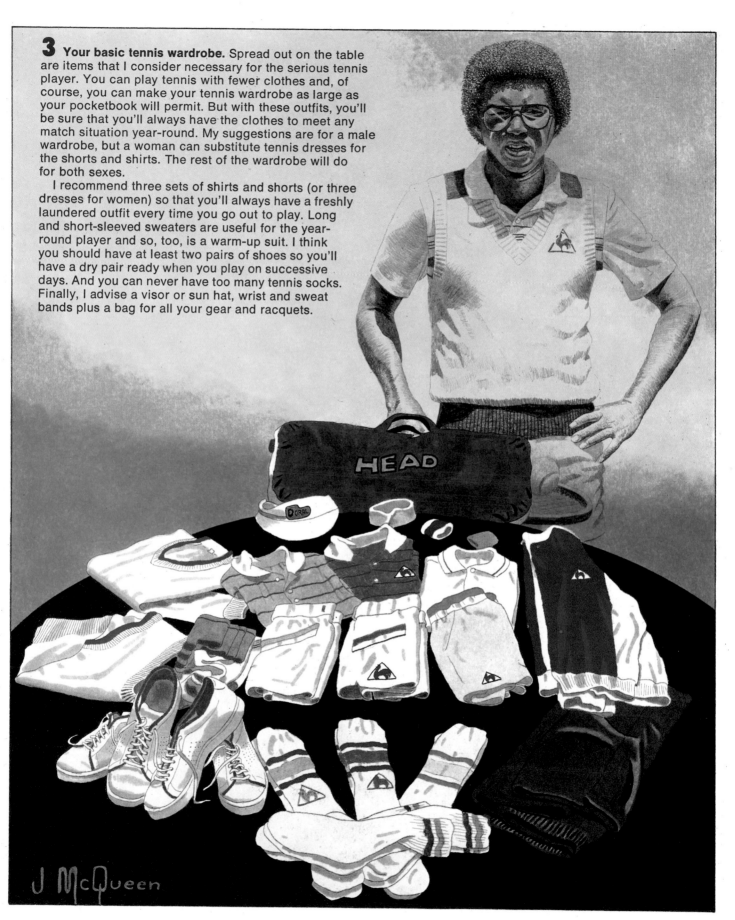

4 **Choosing the right shoes.** Next to your racquet, your shoes are the most important piece of equipment you'll buy. Unless your shoes fit well and support your feet, you won't be comfortable on court. And that can lead to problems, not only with your quality of play, but with sores and blisters—to say nothing of more serious foot problems. I recommend the best leather tennis shoes you can afford. The most supple and supportive shoes are made from a full-grain leather—ask your pro about them. Look for shoes that have a firm heel counter and a substantial arch support. Make sure that the lacing pulls the shoe comfortably around your foot and that there is no movement of your foot inside the shoe as you test it in the store.

5 **Consider an orthotic support.** Even if you don't have foot problems, your game will probably be helped if you put a specially designed orthotic support inside your shoe. This device will align your foot, ankle and lower leg properly to reduce the stress on your muscles as you play. It will also provide a firm arch support. How do you obtain an orthotic support? After you have purchased your shoes, go to a podiatrist who specializes in orthotics and have him make you a pair of supports. They'll cost $150 to $200, but they'll last you many years— and pay off in terms of foot comfort and lessened susceptibility to injury on court over the years. Put the support in your shoes every time you play. You may even want to use them in street shoes when you realize the difference they make in foot comfort.

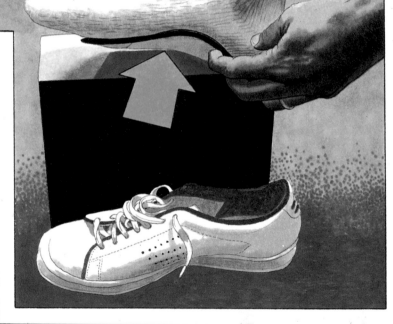

6 **Put your feet in the best socks.** You can add immeasurably to your foot comfort by using the best tennis socks you can find. I wear a thin cotton sock topped by a plush cotton/polyester combination sock. The cotton innersock absorbs perspiration easily while the outer sock insulates and cushions my foot. If you suffer from blisters, use "moleskin"—a soft fabric patch available from your pharmacy—to surround the blister and protect it from further abrasion. A good quality foot powder will help keep your feet drier and free from infection. I believe in pampering my feet because they take an incredible amount of punishment on the court. Do the same for your feet, and your footwork will hold up better.